Wealth Shift

Wealth Shift

Profit Strategies for Investors
as the Baby Boomers Approach Retirement

CHRISTOPHER D. BROOKE, CFM

A Perigee Book

THE BERKLEY PUBLISHING GROUP
Published by the Penguin Group
Penguin Group (USA) Inc.
375 Hudson Street, New York, New York 10014, USA
Penguin Group (Canada), 90 Eglinton Avenue East, Suite 700, Toronto, Ontario M4P 2Y3, Canada
(a division of Pearson Penguin Canada Inc.)
Penguin Books Ltd., 80 Strand, London WC2R 0RL, England
Penguin Group Ireland, 25 St. Stephen's Green, Dublin 2, Ireland (a division of Penguin Books Ltd.)
Penguin Group (Australia), 250 Camberwell Road, Camberwell, Victoria 3124, Australia
(a division of Pearson Australia Group Pty. Ltd.)
Penguin Books India Pvt. Ltd., 11 Community Centre, Panchsheel Park, New Delhi—110 017, India
Penguin Group (NZ), cnr. Airborne and Rosedale Roads, Albany, Auckland 1310, New Zealand
(a division of Pearson New Zealand Ltd.)
Penguin Books (South Africa) (Pty.) Ltd., 24 Sturdee Avenue, Rosebank, Johannesburg 2196,
South Africa
Penguin Books Ltd., Registered Offices: 80 Strand, London WC2R 0RL, England

PRINTING HISTORY
Perigee trade paperback edition / January 2006

ISBN: 0-399-53228-5

PERIGEE is a registered trademark of Penguin Group (USA) Inc.
The "P" design is a trademark belonging to Penguin Group (USA) Inc.

This book has been cataloged by the Library of Congress

PRINTED IN THE UNITED STATES OF AMERICA

10   9   8   7   6   5   4   3   2   1

Dedication

For Sean Fitzpatrick, who urged me to begin.

And for my wife, Missi, who made sure I did not stop.

Table of Contents

Acknowledgments

A number of friends and associates offered themselves as willing readers of *Wealth Shift*'s early drafts, including Sean Fitzpatrick, Brad Galbraith, and my parents, Denny and Barbara Brooke. I'm grateful to each for their varied and valuable opinions.

My lovely wife, Missi and our sons, Tyler and Bradley, have had the front row seats as *Wealth Shift* was developed. Their continued applause is appreciated, as were their occasional heckles.

Andrea Cole contributed much of the research that helped reinforce and supplement the book. Justin Smith took over in the later stages and was equally valuable. Debbie Robert's expert transcriptions were invaluable.

Greg Perry helped me shape each page with his editorial skills and his stubborn attention to our readers' core interests. His voice is woven throughout the book. Ours was a true collaboration, and a highlight of my career.

Introduction

These are obvious and certain times that investors are living in today . . . a boringly calm ocean of stable predictability.

I'm not ignoring or dismissing the presence of uncertainty, both here and abroad. The frightening potential of terrorism, epidemics, and other geo-political disturbances can't be completely counted out as investors look ahead. And market predictions will always be unreliable on a day-to-day, week-to-week basis. But for American investors making long-term decisions about their portfolios, the next fifteen years or so bring one of the most predictable series of events that our economy has ever experienced.

It's a set course. And demographics are driving.

The first wave of baby boomers *will* be retiring and leaving the workforce beginning in 2008, when they turn sixty-two years old. And with them begins a migration of wealth that no economy has experienced on the same scale. Nothing even comes close.

The generation that reshaped America through their restlessness, ingenuity, and sheer mass is about to clock out. While their ability to steer fashion and music has lessened considerably, their power to drive the financial environment is about to enter a wild final lap.

And everybody around them—older, younger, and similarly aged—is going to be taken along.

Because when this generation starts feeling and acting differently about their assets, from their stock portfolios to their homes to their pocket money, everything is going to change. Trillions of dollars will be undergoing an expected and historically documented shift from wealth accumulation to wealth preservation. This is the wealth shift that forms the book's title, and while the demographics can be understood, the environment they create will be filled with dangers and opportunities alike.

My intent with this book is to bring the specific dangers into focus—to help you see what can happen when a massive group within an economy alters its spending patterns. On a smaller scale, it already has happened in past generations and in other countries.

But *Wealth Shift* isn't a history lesson as much as it is strategic guidance on keeping your own hard-earned wealth safe and secure, and helping you uncover substantial opportunities to add to it.

History, Predications, and Practical Guidance

Wealth Shift is organized to first introduce you to the demographic facts at the core of the coming shift in wealth. We will travel through what I've called the "Consumer Spending Progression" in an exercise that demonstrates that the boomers' spending patterns have already dominated the U.S. consumer economy. In this chapter, you'll discover historical analogies to the Great Depression and the effect that a massive immigrant retirement wave had on the economic events of the 1930s.

In the second chapter of the book, you will see a clear picture of what this near future will look like. The consequences of the baby boomers' change in spending patterns will affect the real estate markets, the equities markets, and the bond markets. Taxation policies will begin failing to deliver needed revenue. And institutions from the corner bank to the Federal Reserve will struggle under new financial realities. These are sobering words, but they will help you understand the full consequences of the boomers' next phase of life.

In the chapters that follow, you'll find the reasons why you probably bought the book to begin with: what to do about it all. Cautions and opportunities for growth investors and income investors are defined and explored. International investment strategies are presented for both growth and income investors. Strategies for home ownership and investing in real estate are all presented. Each set of strategic guidelines is contextualized with the very different economic environment of the mid- to late 2000s and beyond.

These guidelines have been developed and honed over a decade of study on demographic and spending patterns, and through a career of creating investment strategies and financial plans for all types of investors, from Fortune 500 executives to business owners to ordinary people just trying to put together a comfortable retirement. You will find valuable knowledge here, no matter what your life goals and situation are.

Wealth Shift Ahead

The American economy has created a broadly based wealth that is without precedent in human history. American business has displayed a remarkable efficiency at production, distribution, marketing, and service. Business makes the vehicles—be they SUVs, DVDs, or mutual funds—and American consumers are driving them—their spending is responsible for roughly two thirds of this nation's economic activity.

It's been a thrilling ride with the boomers up front, yet waiting just down the road is a sharp and potentially treacherous turn in the form of a momentous demographic' event.

Like a major truck accident on the highway, the Wealth Shift will be an awesome and frightening event, with repercussions extending much farther out than the shattered cargo falls. This is not something to anticipate with relish. It may be something to fear. It's definitely something to plan for.

This is the mission of *Wealth Shift*, to help investors see the dangers ahead, the paths to safety, and the opportunities to emerge stronger on the other side.

We begin now.

Christopher D. Brooke
August 2003

The Wealth Shift, Year by Year

Years: 2000 · 2001 · 2002 · 2003 · 2004 · **2005** · 2006 · 2007 · 2008 · 2009 · **2010** · 2011 · 2012 · 2013 · 2014 · **2015** · 2016 · 2017 · 2018 · 2019 · **2020**

Timeline markers:
- First Boomers turn 60 (2006)
- Boomers retire in force / First Boomers turn 62 (2008)
- First Echo Boomers turn 35 / First Boomers turn 65 (2011)
- First Boomers turn 70 (2016)

Retirement
- Boomers retire in massive numbers (~2010)

Equities
- Last opportunity for broad market gains (~2005)
- Shift emphasis to dividend-paying companies, and boomer-driven sectors (~2007)
- Return to broader market strength (~2015)

Fixed Income
- Look for opportunities to capture yields before pressures erode them (~2007)
- Lower grades and lower yields. Use caution with corporates and even municipals (~2012)
- Fewer issues and continued depressed yields (~2013)

Real Estate
- Migration to the South, Southwest, and other retiree-friendly areas (~2005)
- Low rates and depressed home process: Great opportunities for home-buying Echo Boomers (~2008)
- Home prices return with strengthening economy and maturing echo boom market (~2016)

Economy
- Steady growth of corporate earnings, consumer spending, and GDP (~2004)
- Difficult times: Minimal growth in consumer spending impacts entire economy (~2009)
- Stabilizing period, marked by slow growth (~2011)
- Expansion on the strength of echo boomers and their spending (~2015)

Social Security
- Steadily increasing pressure on congress and administration (~2008)
- The pressure mounts. Boomers in a difficult retirement will fill the media (~2013)
- Situation critical (~2019)

Interest Rates
- Downward pressure as boomer borrowers stay away from banks (~2007)
- Rates stabilize as echo boomers' demand for cash grows (~2012)

Chapter 1

Demographics are destiny and money is personal: How we got here

People are so predictable.

They are born, grow up, get old, and die. From person to person, only the details are different. And when observed as a population through the practice of demographics, individual differences—no matter how interesting or entertaining—are simply irrelevant.

But demography gives us more than a snapshot of a population's age. It also offers insight into associated changes in behavior—and that's where investors should start paying careful attention.

The occasional octogenarian skydiver aside, individual *behavior* at each phase in people's lives is almost as predictable as the ultimate end. In expected sequences, they get married, have families, have careers, and retire. Which means that an entire population's behavior over time can also be predicted—their destiny, if you will, is knowable.

Demographers, actuaries, some politicians, and a growing number of investors already know what the members of a generation are likely to do with their time—and their money—as they move through life.

Spending Is Predictable:
Understanding the Consumer Spending Progression

In looking forward, we can anticipate age-based shifts in a person's behavior—*and that those shifts are directly reflected in spending.*

This is the central argument behind the financial opportunities we'll be exploring in *Wealth Shift*. Spending, whether it's on homes, health care, or mutual funds, is the driving force in the economy. Understand this spending progression, and you have taken the first step in planning for, and profiting from, the coming Wealth Shift.

Let's look quickly at this "Consumer Spending Progression," and then specifically, how the spending of the baby boomers has already defined key shifts in the U.S. economy.

Consumer Spending Progression

	Age 0	10	20	30	40	50	60	70	80	90	100
Preproductive Phase	▮▮										
Pre–Household Formation		▮									
Household Formation		▮									
Childrearing			▮								
Maturing Family				▮							
Pre–Empty Nesters					▮						
Empty Nesters					▮						
Preretirement							▮				
Retirement							▮▮▮▮				
End Stage								▮▮▮			

Spending across a large demographic is predictable even if individual spending is not. The boomers have driven the economy with what they've bought so far in the progression. It will continue in the next stages, with the impact expanding to include not only what they buy, but what they *don't* buy.

Preproductive Phase: The Wonder Years

This, essentially, is childhood—beginning at birth and usually lasting until you leave home. You're living off your parents' income, and until the last few years of the phase, not earning much money yourself. Fortunately, your personal expenditures are also minimal: movie tickets, pizza, a few CDs to listen to in your room.

Your parents, on the other hand, have been shelling it out—starting before you were born and staying steady, and *predictable*, every year you're at home and under their care.

Pre–Household Formation: Young Adults at Work and Play

This begins when the front door closes behind you. You've left home for good.

You might be nineteen or twenty-five. It might be after high school, vocational school, or college. And while it's likely that the readers of *Wealth Shift* went to college and graduated, most people in a given generation do neither.

But everyone, sooner or later, goes to work. You're generating income in your first jobs, and setting the table for your career. These days, career paths are more fluid and less linear, and it's likely that you'll have two or more careers over the course of your work life.

What is predictable is your spending. And for the most part, you don't have a lot of significant fixed expenses. You probably don't have a mortgage yet. Rent, a car payment, groceries, and entertainment are probably the biggest checks you write each month.

There may be a student loan, but unless you're just out of medical school, it's probably a very manageable amount. In fact, it's the people who go to school later in life who have larger loans. Older students don't usually rely on their parents to pick up part of the tuition tab. People who go from high school straight to college tend to borrow less, and have less to repay. Which means there is probably money to spend on a few low-end luxuries. Your first TV and some fashionable clothes . . . a nice stereo . . . an expensive dinner out with lots of forks on the table. To marketers, this is a very desirable population.

They've got some money and a lot of attitude.

Household Formation: New Stuff, New Debt

Now the real world starts to get a little more complicated.

You found a wife or a husband or a domestic partner of some sort, and you've just bought a house, which inherently means you're spending far more than you're earning. Today a young couple may have a combined income of $70,000, and they maybe buy a house for $120,000. In a flurry of signatures, they've just spent nearly two years of income and the house is still empty.

Expenses add up quickly in the household formation phase, but the optimism of youth is at work here, as well as the force of economics: your income is steady and growing. There is a confidence in your ability to repay debts. And judging from the mail each day, the credit card companies have confidence in you, too.

So it's off to the furniture store, the appliance store, and maybe the car dealership on the corner. The milk-crate bookshelves are finally retired, and in their place is a new home entertainment center.

These are significant purchases that usually add to the debt load, and dual-income households seem to add up debt faster than those of singles.

What about savings? In this phase, let's call their savings "deferred spending." The money goes into the savings account, but as soon as a goal is reached—maybe enough for a car down payment or a vacation to Hawaii—the money is spent. It's better than going into debt, but there's probably not much more money going into long-term savings. After all, every household needs stuff.

There is also a presumption here that two people can manage to save more than singles. Not true. As the baby boomers popularized the dual-income couple, savings rates did not increase. In fact, economists saw a decrease in savings rates while dual-income households were forming. To a young couple with two incomes today, there's just no shortage of things to buy. It's the American dream, which can sometimes look more like a nightmare. But that's another book.

And what about the household that is blessed with children, and one of the parents leaves the workforce to raise them? Debt levels stay about the same, and so do the savings. Expenses, however, start to look a lot different, regardless of who's working and who's at home.

Sushi dinners are out. Smashed carrots are in.

Childrearing: Kids Growing, Cash Flowing

Expenses skyrocket when a household is raising children. The expanding household is spending money at the grocery store, the shoe store, the nursery school, and just about everywhere else that sells family staples.

Indeed, debt can climb during childrearing, especially if the expanding family needs a bigger house to fit into. It may be the first, second, or third home purchase, but the fact is, homes are usually not cheaper when they're bigger.

What spending is not happening? Luxury item purchases tend to be deferred. Level-headed parents simply aren't going to buy and display a $2,500 crystal vase with two young sons in the house. Besides, with cash going out so quickly, there are probably not a lot of disposable resources anyway. But there is good news.

Income is growing quickly, as this is one of the most productive periods of a person's career. During the late twenties on through the forties, income accelerates at the steepest rates. Still, for most people, that money is plowed right back into the family, and not handed over to the banker or the broker.

Certainly, the wisest young parents have already started to invest; yet even then, their investment priorities are more likely to be saving for their children's college versus their own retirement. And why worry? Retirement is thirty years away and their careers are really beginning to gain some financial traction. There will be plenty of time and money to save and invest later.

Right now, it's karate lessons, computer camp, and vacations to Disneyland.

Maturing Family: Hungry Teenagers

For many families, this phase is the site of a fortunate intersection: expenses are beginning to decline—or the end is in sight as the children get closer to leaving home—and income is flowing now as they enter the peak earning years. They're experienced, productive, and healthy.

During their maturing family phase of the spending progression, people are at or near their career pinnacles. Good thing, too, because expenses have stayed high as well—maybe another home, a few more luxury goods, a car and insurance for the new driver or drivers, and the groceries! Have you ever seen a species that consumed more product than teenagers?

Depending on the years that separate the children, this phase can happen quickly, or it can be divided into its own phases as each child leaves. And while college costs can be a serious drag on the family finances, retirement is becoming a real issue, not a vague concept.

So retirement saving and investing move to the forefront here. Regardless of why maturing families are investing, the priority is growth—not preservation. Tolerance for risk is almost certainly higher now than in the decades to follow.

Meanwhile, the 401(k) is building, and the performance of the IRA is getting more attention when the statement arrives.

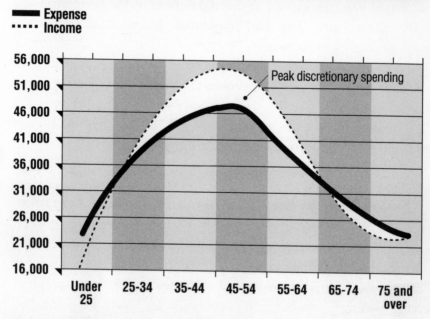

Consumer Income vs. Expenditure

━━━ **Expense**
• • • • **Income**

Peak discretionary spending

| | Under 25 | 25-34 | 35-44 | 45-54 | 55-64 | 65-74 | 75 and over |

56,000
51,000
46,000
41,000
36,000
31,000
26,000
21,000
16,000

There's a sweet spot for most people where income outpaces expenses. But the leading edge of the boomers, which includes millions of people, are moving into a period of decreased spending.

U.S. Statistical Abstract

Pre–Empty Nesters: Seeing the Light, and Shopping for It, Too

This is when the children are actually off to college or their post–high school education, but not financially independent. They could even still be living at home, but by now have some work skills that reduce their drain on the family resources.

Kids in college can cost a fortune, but this is what the parents have been saving for, so the cash outlay may be easily manageable. After all, they are making more money than ever.

So much in fact, that in this phase we start to see that nagging debt finally worked down. Savings goes up with the reduced debt service, and the focus shifts off college savings and fully onto retirement accounts. Plus, the kids aren't camped in front of the refrigerator. It's quiet in the house. The only thing breaking the silence is the extra change jingling in pockets.

There may be a wedding to pay for, or some help in getting the kids set up in their own households, but discretionary income is at a significant level.

New built-in lights would look wonderful in the bedroom, and wouldn't it be great to see Paris . . .

Empty Nesters: Peak Earnings and Reduced Expenses

It's not just midlife; it's a financial crossover too. After a period of extraordinarily high expenses—tuition, housing, and a dorm full of expenses—there's a sudden and welcome decrease. Is that a sigh of relief I hear?

The kids may be stopping back home for a year or two while their careers take hold, but they are adults now and able to pay for more, also creating more: more time and more money.

For people in this age group, expenses may be lower than they've been in many years, while income is the highest it may ever be. This should be when retirement investing takes priority. But in reality, retirement investing often shares the shopping list with luxury goods.

A luxury good for one empty nester is going to be different than the next empty nester—it could be a new Porsche or a used RV—but with income at its peak, there's usually room for both some luxury and some savings. Chances are, though, the money saved simply is not enough.

There's still time, and hopefully good health, but the clock is ticking. They'll pass on that IPO, and buy some more blue chips.

The opposite of this mindset is evident as well. Many investors feel they have to be significantly more aggressive here since their failure to save has put them behind. They feel like they're behind the eight ball. Which they are.

Preretirement: Steady Progress or Panic

Here, the luxury spending tends to drop and the saving and investing take on a singular goal: retirement. At this phase you may see people saving as much as 25–50 percent of their income. If the house isn't paid for, it usually happens here. If the debts are still around, they are eliminated here. Bonuses that people used to spend go straight into savings or their investments.

This can be a time of satisfied anticipation or anxious maneuvering. Is there enough? Where will we live? Do we really need those season tickets?

The mindset and behavior are conservative. Tolerance for risk, which has been gradually eroding, is bottoming out. They can't absorb any setbacks now.

Sell the technology stocks. Buy some bonds.

Of course, some people just can't step away from the table. They try to maximize return until the day they retire, and the 2000–2002 bear market was a disaster for these people.

Retirement: Conservative, Careful, and Caring

Retirement can be a wonderful time, full of exploration and friendship. Or it can be shaped by rigid frugality. Either way, and at every stage in between, this is a conservative time.

For the retirees who have planned well and generated adequate wealth, spending tends to migrate to recreation and comfort purchases . . . things like golf and restaurants. A Kenyan safari may not be on the calendar, but a trip to Branson, Missouri, or Las Vegas may be coming up next month.

Maintaining good health is a primary focus, which shifts considerable spending over to prescription medications and other general health care expenses. For a person whose health is failing, nearly every purchase can be related to health care.

The good news is that life expectancy is climbing every year, and more and more people are living quite healthy lives into their eighties and beyond. To fill their time, many retirees are also filling their hearts. Volunteerism tends to pick up in retirement, maybe in a school, a hospital, a political convention, or a boardroom. Either way, they have a lot to offer and every institution is right to make room for their involvement.

As for their investment style, forget the biotech. In fact, you might not find any equities at all. Fixed-return asset instruments tend to replace appreciating assets. The prominent behavior here is identifying income opportunities: if it doesn't guarantee a return, it's probably already been sold. And this, once again, is a critical fact to understand as we anticipate the approaching Wealth Shift.

Living with a Pay Cut, Are You Ready?

One rule of thumb that has guided retirement planning for years is the Sixty Percent Rule. It states that during each year of a healthy retirement, you'll need sixty percent of your annual income. That's bunk.

Sure, some people do it. But not by choice. How many people really want to take a forty percent pay cut the day they need all their money.

Now this isn't a retirement planning guide—there's a lot of good advice on bookshelves and in the offices of planners everywhere. But I have seen that people who properly prepare for retirement wind up pending significantly more than they did just prior to retirement.

Think about it: what expenses actually go down by not working? Maybe some clothing expenses, or commuting-related costs, but for the most part when you're working, you're not spending your own money.

Now, all of a sudden, you have twenty-four hours to fill— let's go to dinner, let's go on a trip, let's go see Aunt Margaret in Florida. Heck, let's move to Florida.

You get the idea, but are you ready for the reality?

End Game: Money in Motion Again

At the end of life, remaining assets take on a special power and potential. This is when many people turn to philanthropy, even on a modest scale. And, of course, the rest of the family is watching very carefully, if not offering their . . . guidance.

Moving money across generations is fraught with pitfalls. Timing is critical, and decisions are often delayed until the last possible day.

Needless to say, when you're lying in bed wondering how much to keep for your needs and how much to give away to your treasured institutions and favorite niece, you're not going to be gambling with your money. At least not on Wall Street.

Along for the Ride with the Baby Boomers

Large groups of age-aligned consumers have a big influence on the rest of the economy. They influence what's on the market, what the market price will be, and how much producers will bring to market. We know this happens because it already has.

The first time in U.S. history that a group had this kind of impact on the economy took place from the late 1800s until the early 1930s. They were immigrants, mostly from Europe, and we'll explore their influence later in the book. In advance, we can say they changed how our young country worked, ate, and entertained itself. And when a vast majority of them neared retirement age, and became more conservative in their spending behavior, it was about 1929.

Yet no group of consumers has had more influence on the American markets than the baby boomers. This is old news to all but the most economically naive. And yet, many investors have simply watched the boomers approach retirement they way someone watching the Weather Channel in Omaha might experience a hurricane approaching Miami: "Troubling, but what can be done?"

Plenty. But before we get to strategies, allow me to demonstrate the specific effect that the boomers have had on the economy as they moved through the Consumer Spending Progression. They changed everything then. They'll do it again. But first, who are they?

They Are Massive

Approximately 76 million people were born in America in the eighteen years (1946–1964) that followed World War II. Now add in the immigrants who are also born during that time and now living in the U.S., and the number of people in midlife or nearing retirement swells even further.

They Are Rich

The boomers own big homes, expensive cars, and fat investment portfolios. Every month, a mountain of statements drop from banks and brokerage houses reminding them just how much money they can count on for retirement.

What those statements don't say is how much the U.S. economy, if not the global economy, is counting on that money, too.

The Sharpest Edges of an Eighteen-Year Boom

While the baby boomers are spread out over eighteen years, there are two subsets of this group that are most important to marketers and investors.

The oldest boomers—the ones born from 1946 to 1949—are the trailblazers. As they entered different phases of the Consumer Spending Progression, they began to influence the rest of the country, be it diaper manufacturers or record labels.

When the first boomers were born, baby food manufacturers were caught completely by surprise. Demand outstripped supply, so prices went up dramatically—the classic inflation model. By the time production and distribution caught up with demand, the boom was rolling and prices stabilized. Gerber, a sleepy little baby food maker, was suddenly a powerful national brand, not because of their killer business plan, but because of demographics.

The point is, you don't have to wait for the entire group to move through a single phase before significant shifts occur. It's true of babies and retirees.

The second part of the boom investors need to pay careful attention to is the largest part, in terms of sheer numbers.

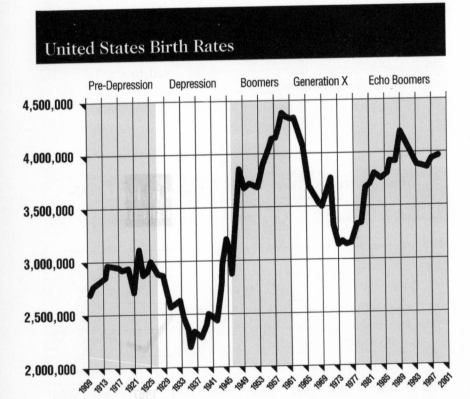

United States Birth Rates

The numbers can't be ignored by investors. The baby boom sent a shock wave through the American culture, and they're not through yet.

U.S. Census Data

As you can see from the chart, the baby boom made the loudest noise from about 1949 to 1959. This was the birth of their cultural and economic muscle. Let's look at what has happened as they've flexed it through the Consumer Spending Progression, picking up the story when they had some money in their pockets.

Preproductive Boomers: Rebels with Rhythm

Much has been written on the young people of the 1960s. They challenged political establishments. They rejected social norms. They reimagined personal freedom. It's essentially the same thing all young adults do; it's just that there were so many of them in the 1960s that the rest of the nation, and the world, was forced to pay attention. They also bought a lot of records.

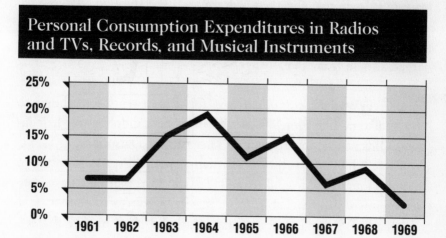

Personal Consumption Expenditures in Radios and TVs, Records, and Musical Instruments

Spending on music and entertainment took a big share of the young boomers' wallets. That helped make music a big business.

U.S. Statistical Abstract

15

As the chart shows, sales of music and music products made a dramatic upturn during the early 1960s—it's no coincidence that the trailblazing boomers were entering their teenaged years. Same with TVs and other low-end luxuries that are the typical purchases for the preproductive phase.

Demographically tuned-in investors in the early 1960s would have seen the trend and started buying stocks in music companies and denim makers and, of course, Volkswagen dealerships.

Prehousehold Boomers: Spending Toward Adulthood

In the late 1960s, the first wave of boomers starts to form their households. By the early 1970s, pre–household formation is reaching noticeable momentum.

Who noticed first? Japan, for one.

That's because they already had been through it. The Japanese baby boom happened before the war (as is usually the case with expansionist nations), and they had already lived through a large wave of young people moving through a Consumer Spending Progression. They knew that this group was going to need a lot of cars, and they targeted them from an early age.

Japanese manufacturers were ready with plenty of small, durable, low-priced commuter cars for these twenty-somethings to buy and trade like Hot Wheels. These people didn't want their father's Oldsmobiles or Plymouths. They wanted Datsuns.

The same can be said for Germany, another expansionist nation that also knew how to make small cars and vans that may have been lacking in consistent reliability, but not in appeal.

Datsun, Mazda, and Toyota captured a huge market share— and they have kept many of those customers for the next forty years. The Lexus, Acura, and Infiniti luxury cars they drive now carry the automotive DNA of those early, perfectly timed little beaters. And who is buying the new Beetle? Sales numbers show it's as many baby boomers as it is young adults.

Another bit of good timing. The boomers never fought with Japan or Germany. The products coming out of those countries weren't seen through the same red, white, and blue lenses that the WWII generation wore. Japanese zero fighter planes were powered by Nissan engines, long before the Datsun name was crafted to appeal to American buyers. But to the young people buying them, the only zeros that mattered were in their payment books and maintenance expenses.

Boomers Forming Households: Inflation Moves in, Too

When the boomers start buying homes and forming households in large numbers, the first evidence of inflation appears. Inflation is essentially what occurs when too much money is chasing too few goods.

In the 70s there were not enough homes and not enough corn flakes. There was a huge demand for all consumer goods, and production and distribution simply weren't prepared. Could they have been? Not really.

People will blame the 70s inflation on Vietnam or the OPEC oil embargo. Oil clearly had an inflationary presence, but it wasn't as significant as the simple fact that almost thirty percent of the nation was entering their household formation phase. Lots of competition for very few goods, and prices went up.

If you're of a certain age, you might remember President Ford's "WIN" campaign—Whip Inflation Now—complete with buttons and media reports. Yet, short of having lots of homes built in advance and warehouses filled with yet-to-be-demanded goods, there was nothing that have could have been done in the 70s to avoid inflation.

The other hot product of the 70s was money. Loans to the boomers were being booked at record rates, record interest rates, too.

Then, in the early 80s, as the later baby boomers started to enter these same phases, why didn't the costs go up? Because production had adapted to those initial baby boomers. Producers increased capacity until eventually they were producing too many goods. That happened in the mid 80s and we started to see inflation reduced. So it wasn't anything that Paul A. Volker did . . . or the Fed, or the President. They had almost nothing to do with lowering inflation; it had been predestined from thirty years before.

Boomer Parents: New Kids on the Very Expensive Block

As we entered the late 70s and early 80s, the boomers began to have their children. Spending and debt stayed at very high levels and homes became an absolute necessity. If the newlyweds and young married couples could do fine in a rental, the new parents could not.

Right in step, then, housing prices begin to rise, especially in the densely populated large metropolitan areas of the United States: New York, Boston, Chicago, Los Angeles, and Dallas. Housing prices in these cities took a sharp turn upward. After all, most people are going to live and buy houses near where they grew up. Some will be anxious to leave, especially college graduates. But for many of those, returning home is how they begin their careers.

Remember, this isn't anecdotal. This is demographics. Millions and millions of people all doing about the same thing and spending in about the same ways. Now collect a sizable percentage of those millions around certain areas, **and what happened was entirely predictable. The same can be said for what the boomers are moving toward: it is predictable.**

Maturing Boomer Households: Stable Lives and Stable Rates

Throughout the 80s and early 90s, baby boomers were somewhere in their maturing family phase. Inflation was a memory, and the savings rates were starting to climb.

Depending on how closely spaced the kids came, this phase could span from fifteen to twenty-five years, making it more difficult to ascribe a specific economic shift to their spending. But one statistic does stand out: home sales away from the large eastern and western metro areas. Suddenly, homebuilders in states like Iowa, Minnesota, and Ohio couldn't keep up with demand. The Midwest was swimming in boomer families from larger cities who were seeking better schools, easier commutes, and safer streets. Granted, some of this growth was homegrown and some was fueled by corporate reassignments, but once the city slickers got settled in, they stayed, and they kept spending.

Empty Nester Boomers: Spending Through the Pain

Throughout the 90s, but especially during the last half of that decade, the baby boomers sent their babies out into the world. Finally, there's money to save, invest, and spend on the kinds of luxury goods every boomer deserves.

Those early boomers hit fifty in 1996, and every day another 10,000 or so joined them in the half-century club. Turning fifty is a bummer; they had to do something, and spending is what they know best.

Luxury purchases started to accelerate in the 90s. Home remodeling, jewelry, luxury travel, and fine dining all saw steep growth curves. And once again, the Japanese carmakers saw the boomers coming before their domestic competition did. Lexus was formed by Toyota, along with Infiniti by Nissan and Acura by Honda. They knew the American public was just about to jump into the luxury spending stage of their lives.

This discretionary spending wasn't only on luxury, however; it was also saved and invested. This bull market continued to generate higher and higher returns as buckets of money poured in until the overvalued internet stocks finally tumbled and took the rest of the market down. Then terrorists effectively shut down the comeback in 2001. But let's focus on the boomers' investing in the 1990s. It was driving the market up then, and it will be driving it in the future.

Boomers were pouring money into equities, through their 401(k)—through mutual funds—through their brokers, their advisors, and their next-door neighbor's cousin's friend. Everyone was winning on Wall Street for a number of reasons. Certainly, the electronic revolution had made companies vastly more efficient, and thus a better value. And the purveyors of electronic solutions were going public and getting rich creating the goods that improved efficiency.

Still, an essential truth about investing in stocks (at least short-term) has almost nothing to do with an individual company's performance. You see, rising stock prices simply means there are more motivated buyers than sellers. And the baby boomers were all on the phone (or online) shouting (or clicking) "buy" and rarely "sell."

Yo-Yos on the Hill: Short-Term Cycles Will Always Exist

Wealth Shift is not a tool for predicting recessions or short-term boom cycles. Those will always occur within large-scale demographic movements. Inventories are going to grow. They're going to shrink, then they'll grow again.

Short-term business and production cycles, as well as political events, can't be reliably predicted by economists or investors. And trying can make you crazy, or at least dizzy.

You see, overemphasis on short-term cycling is like watching a kid walk up a hill playing with a yo-yo. You can watch the yo-yo, or you can watch the kid's progress.

In *Wealth Shift*, as well as my private practice, we're watching the kid.

Early 2000s: The Boomer Truck Is Racing Ahead, Right on Track

By now, you can see the spending patterns unfold and get a sense of their economic consequences. They were predictable from the day the boomers were born, and predictable spending behavior trends are going to continue in the near future and the long-term future. Moreover, we're all pretty much along for the ride. Where the boomers go, the country follows, and not just in economic terms but in political, social, and cultural terms as well. In the next section, let's take a quick look at the ride so far.

Political Influence, Then . . .

Winston Churchill once said, "If you're not a liberal by the time you're twenty you have no heart. And if you are not a conservative by the time you are forty, you likely have no brain."

Given that truism, would the absolutely necessary advances in civil and women's rights have taken place without the passions of millions of young, liberal-leaning activists? Certainly not at the rate they took place in the 60s and 70s. The problems had existed for decades. But it took a critical mass of young people to attack the injustices and force the governments and other institutions—including business—to change.

They weren't brighter or more ambitious; there were simply so many of them. They fed off of each other's energy, so that some wonderful changes occurred in the political landscape in the 1960s and 70s.

Then, in the 1970s and 80s, we saw changes in family formation. We saw dual-income couples, with some wives making more than the husbands; we saw single parents making it on their own.

Private retirement plans were born during this time as well. The first IRA, with all its federal tax breaks, was created by Congress in 1981. Why? Boomers made enough noise about their need to save without being taxed that the government listened. They had to—an election is always around the corner.

Political Influence, Now

As the boomers enter the empty nest preretirement phases, they have turned more conservative, taking the whole country with them. Heck, Democrats today are more conservative than the Republicans were in the 1960s.

Now taxes and social security are big issues, and these folks vote. It's why the estate tax has now been revised. It hadn't been revised in twenty years, now it's been revised three times in four years and it's going to be revised every year until 2010. Clearly, the baby boomers are concerned about retirement and downright worried about their inheritance.

In general, tolerance is out—along with expensive welfare programs. Conservatism and tax aversion are in.

Influence in Detroit

When the boomers were raising their own families in the 80s and 90s, the Plymouth GTO was not the top-selling model. It was

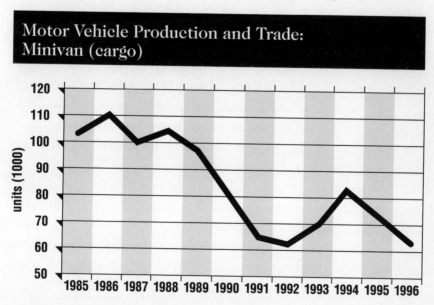

Motor Vehicle Production and Trade: Minivan (cargo)

Minivan sales collapsed when the early-stage boomers moved out of the "soccer mom" stage. Their kids were becoming teenagers and these vehicles didn't fit with the boomers' family needs any longer.

U.S. Statistical Abstract

the minivan, a category essentially created for the boomers. Detroit was finally getting it.

Muscle cars weren't rolling off many lines anywhere, here or in Japan. Nissan got rid of the critically acclaimed 300ZX; Toyota got rid of the Supra. The Corvette went through a comical identity crisis.

Now, feeling nostalgic, boomers are buying retro. Roadsters and Beetles. Honda has a convertible that was engineered so as not to mess up the driver's hair. The boomers once again are determining what the rest of us had to choose from.

Influence Over Health Care

Boomer women demanded a way to have children later in life, and their numbers prompted medicine (and medical businesspeople) to respond with fertility treatments. Now fertility medicine is among the most profitable fields for a new physician to enter, at least for a while.

The medical field that continues to grow, (or should I say, reduce), is cosmetic surgery. Liposuction, face-lifts, vein treatments—you name it, and the boomers are paying for it. The ads and the clinics are appearing as fast as the wrinkles.

A friend in the pharmaceutical industry told me there was an efficacious drug treatment for erectile dysfunction on the shelf in the 1970s. But where was the market? Viagra debuted in 1996 in response to the demands of aging men and their partners who refused to simply hide their frustrations. Okay, fine, they aren't twenty anymore. But they are a potent market.

Cultural Influence

I'm not a music critic, but I can read the charts that indicate one kind of musical success: sales. Young people will always dominate the record stores, but the concert venues are offered to bands that can put the most cheeks in the seats. The most profitable touring acts of the early 2000s include Jimmy Buffett, the Eagles, Billy Joel, Elton John, The Rolling Stones, Kiss, and other bands of the boomers' youth.

They fill the expensive seats (every inch of them now), and they buy the expensive merchandise. There are only so many nights a year in only so many venues, and the boomers are deciding what the rest of the nation can listen to on any given night. They aren't in the band, but they are setting the rhythm.

Here's the bottom line: age determines spending, and spending en masse determines the direction of the economy. The good news for forward-looking investors is that age is about as certain as . . . well, death and taxes.

The goal here was to establish the economic might of the baby boomer generation. Their predictable, age-based spending is driving the economy. The looming question is what's going to happen when they stop working and start spending money like retired people. They will save differently. They will invest differently.

And sharp investors who see the shift coming will change right along with them.

Chapter 2

Feeling the Shift: Institutions Under Stress

When individual spending shifts, it's not just the merchants who must absorb the change. The demographic movement away from working, growth investing, and borrowing will unleash electoral pressures and market forces strong enough to shake the institutions of government and finance. The Federal Reserve, the Social Security Administration, Congress, your local government, and the corner bank will all be rattled. The only question is, how hard?

The changing spending patterns and demographic forces that we've already discussed will be doing the shaking—from automotive purchasing trends to preferred investment vehicles. By now, it should be clear: what the boomers want, they usually get. Commercial markets are more nimble in their response (the boomers' dollars always get their attention), but governments can be turned as well—often too late for the leaders in the change efforts to reap the benefits, but turned nevertheless. Take the Family Leave Act, for example.

In early 1993, President Clinton signed the Family and Medical Leave Act (FMLA), which allows people to take time off from work to care for their families or themselves while creating a federal law that protects their job.

Before this law was enacted, many American employees were unable to take time off from work to care for a child or in family emergencies, for fear of losing their jobs. In fact, according to the U.S. Bureau of Labor Statistics, in 1990 less than forty percent of all women working for companies of 100 employees or more were eligible for unpaid maternity leave upon the birth of a child.

The signing of this act was the culmination of a struggle that had gone on for nearly a decade. And who was writing the letters, working the phones, and generally shaping the debate? Baby boomer mothers and fathers with young children were at the committee hearings and on the Capitol-step rallies. They were the public face and the behind-the-scenes force.

By the time the law was enacted in 1993, the largest group of baby boomers was, for the most part, through the period of their lives with young children at home. Yet, as with so many good ideas they helped to turn into good policy—the laws and policies on sexual harassment come to mind as well—the people coming behind them stood to benefit the most.

Consumers in the Voting Booth

The skeptical reader (my favorite kind) will object to the notion that age concentration in a population is not enough to counter the well-funded, well-organized lobbies that represent the various business interests in Washington, D.C. True, industry groups and their various lobbyists are spending their way into offices, hearing rooms, and bills. But industries aren't the only groups with high-performance lobbies.

One of the most organized and well-funded lobbies is the AARP, which, by the way, no longer stands for the American Association of Retired People. Now AARP stands for, well . . . nothing really, and that's quite intentional. In simply going by its well-known acronym, the AARP keeps its muscle in Washington, without limiting its membership to those old, "retired" people. You can join AARP when you turn fifty. The organization is strong, smart, and effective. It also counts over 32 million people as members. When the AARP calls a congressman's office, that congressman or woman takes the call—even if he or she has to put Big Oil on hold to do it.

In fact, the only consumer lobbies with real influence to craft a law are the ones with a lot of baby boomer members, like the people organized to enact a Patients' Bill of Rights. Could this legislation have even hailed a cab in D.C., much less made it to the Senate floor, if it weren't for the baby boomers' mounting frustrations with managed care organizations?

Another powerful truth on the side of the baby boomers is the fact that industries and their organizations don't vote. They pay candidates' campaign bills and can even make them dance once elected, but organizations don't pull the lever. People do, and voting statistics indicate that older people vote at higher percentages than younger voters. Moreover, they carry very specific issues with them into the voting booth. No prospective senator or congressman wants these people voting against them.

My point is that, both by determination and sheer numbers, the baby boomers have forced institutions to bend. During the Wealth Shift, we'll see just how far they can go. Let's explore the very real possibilities.

Stress in the U.S. Treasury

America's savings account has been posting some impressive and comforting numbers. In 2002, the U.S. Treasury collected some $1.6 trillion dollars, which is right in line with past years' collections. The cash has been arriving steadily as the baby boomers earn higher incomes and move into higher tax brackets.

Revenue from individual income tax amounts to approximately two thirds of the U.S. Treasury's annual take. And the tax rates that moved higher and higher to fund the Cold War did not come down with the Berlin Wall. The so-called peace dividend was absorbed into government just like a family's budget might absorb the payoff of a car loan. The kids' allowances didn't go up, but the money got spent on something else. Beginning in 2008 there will be less and less of it to spend.

The first baby boomers turn sixty-two that year, and the retirement parade begins. Every single day of that year, and for years and years to follow, between 8,000 and 10,000 baby boomers will clock out. Every day, another 8,000 to 10,000 people take their earned incomes away from the Treasury's reach. How much? Demographers put the baby boomers' average income on retirement day at approximately $54,000.

While $54,000 might seem modest to the readers of *Wealth Shift*, the individual number isn't as important as the total. Every day, between $432,000,000 and $540,000,000 in personal income will drop from the economy and evaporate as a source of revenue to the Treasury. That's *every day*.

What's replacing it? During the period beginning in 2008, approximately 7,000 to 9,000 people will join the workforce each day, each earning less than $30,000 per year. And because of our graduated tax rates, most of these new income earners are going to be in lower tax brackets.

The bottom line is that we're going to have a lot of high-tax-rate earners leaving the system and being replaced by 10 to 20 percent less, earning half as much, taxed at half the rate. The country's net taxable income is going to simply plummet—to fall like a stone kicked off a cliff.

Clearly, retirees may still have taxable income from tax-deferred investments like IRAs. But the tax rate for those people will be much lower than the mid to high thirty percent tax rate or even the low thirty percent or even high twenty percent rates. Try 15 percent, or now the new 10 percent rate. Should they keep working into retirement, they almost certainly won't be bringing home $54,000 taxable dollars like before. And if they are relying on Social Security for most or all of their income (and millions will), they may not pay any tax at all. Zero. Not a bad tax liability but an awful situation for the U.S. Treasury and for the nation as a whole.

There are three possible responses by the Treasury and the Federal government: the first will be to raise taxes wherever they can—on the workers working, on the corporations, on the investments. The second will be to borrow money in the form of government bonds—which also happens to be an ideal instrument for income generation in retirement, to be explored in detail in a later chapter. And the third will be to spend less on programs and entitlements.

Look for all three to occur, and for the rancorous debate each will generate, but let's briefly imagine the most objectionable: taxes.

New Taxes on Retirement Distributions

Imagine how hard it will be for the IRS to keep their hands off the money sitting in IRAs and other retirement accounts. Most industry analysts estimate there will be tens of trillions of dollars in these accounts by 2010. For most investors, distribution of that money is carefully planned so that on any given year, the realized income does not push the investor into a higher tax bracket. But tax laws aren't biblical laws; they can be changed in response to changing conditions. There already is a 10 percent tax penalty now on distributions prior to age 59½. Imagine a similar tax that's collected right off the top, no matter when distribution takes place.

New Capital Gains Taxes

Imagine the temptation to raise the capital gains tax rates that have been successfully whittled down by the boomers and by the officials they helped elect. Even in the bear markets of the early 2000s, people are selling and realizing significant gains. After all, the Dow and NASDAQ shot returns into orbit in the ten years from 1990 to 2000. Retired boomers themselves could push for this change, especially hard since many of their capital gains will have already been realized.

VAT, Estate Taxes, and More

Imagine a national sales tax, or Value Added Tax (VAT). It sounded like a kooky idea when Steve Forbes was preaching it, but it may reenter the national debate with a fresh urgency during the Wealth Shift.

Imagine sharply rising estate taxes. It's no coincidence that this tax started its decline just as the baby boomers were inheriting their parents' wealth. Every vote cast for George W. Bush in 2000 was a vote for this tax reduction, which will supposedly "sundown" in 2011. Will it happen? And if it does, will estate taxes stay low?

Imagine revenuers looking to grab a tax wherever the money is being spent. And during the Wealth Shift, boomers will be spending it on health care. Look for proposals that tax specific health care purchases—a health care "sales tax" of sorts, like a twenty percent excise tax on private pay health care, to pick a possible scenario. That would raise premiums and, in effect, spread the burden. You could also see challenges to the tax-exempt status of many not-for-profit hospitals that have, in fact, been turning a handsome profit.

Naturally, one viable option is to raise the income tax rates for the people still earning an income. Easier said than proposed, debated, drafted, approved, and signed into law. Which brings us to the next stressful place to be when the Wealth Shift hits.

Stress in the Congress

Say whatever else you want about the U.S. Congress, but everyone agrees they are impressive in their ability to spend money. Just about any senator or congressman could have said, "A billion dollars here, a billion dollars there, pretty soon you're talking about real money." Got to love those guys.

But what happens when the money starts to dry up with the drop in income tax revenue and the increase in entitlement spending? Those Social Security checks are going to start going out in very big bundles beginning in 2008. Where will the money come from?

Even with new tax revenue mentioned above and the issuance of debt in the form of bonds, the budgets for all our favorite programs—from weapons systems to school lunches—are likely to shrink, forcing legislators to make some unpleasant choices for all of us.

In 2003, we are once again seeing huge, Cold War–style deficits, and the even larger numbers that are looming and contained in several reports are probably not taking a broad enough view of the impending boomers' retirement. While I join many economists who hold that even high deficit spending can be good for the larger economy (what is home ownership, but deficit spending?), there is a limit to what's healthy. We may cross that limit in the years ahead. Either way, we will definitely see a polarized electorate, with nervous baby boomers on one side and their children—the so-called echo boom—on the other.

Baby Boomers vs. Echo Boomers with Congress in the Middle

With diametrically opposed priorities on the essential matters of taxation and congressional spending, generational skirmishes are virtually certain, and Congress will be called in to referee.

How will Congress appease the boomers who still control most of the wealth, have immediate and acute needs, and vote in great numbers? How will they appease the echo boomers, who will be taking their place as the next generation of voters and wage earners? If you're thinking about political office, think again.

Issue #1 will no doubt be the preservation of the Social Security system. That means higher taxes somehow, somewhere, on someone. Will the echo boomers cheerfully offer to take home less each payday so that retirees can keep their golf club memberships? Probably not. And will boomers submit to some of the taxes discussed earlier so the echo boom can have steak instead of steak burgers? Doubtful.

And what about the people in the demographic middle, the much-maligned Gen X? In that space between two demographic behemoths, no one will hear them scream.

Legislators as Reformers

The pain of change in large institutions is usually softened by its gradualness. Change is methodical and ponderous, and probably an appropriate way to proceed when public trust is at stake. The problem is, there will be no time for pondering. And yet, watch them.

Watch the Congress delay, debate, study, and argue until Social Security is facing insurmountable deficits and extremely painful choices, each with dreadful repercussions. Reform is essential, beginning now.

Watch the Congress wrestle with Medicare and Medicaid. Both programs are already paying doctors and hospitals less than the costs of services—driving down revenue and putting good hospitals at risk. Again, reform is essential.

Watch Congress enact new employment laws that protect older workers from age discrimination while they actively discourage or even outlaw most mandatory retirement laws. Sure, no one wants a seventy-eight-year-old pilot at the controls, but why boot out a wage-earning, tax-paying CEO just because he or she gets age spots? This reform should come easily, but few things are going to be easy in a stressed-out Congress.

Stress in the Federal Reserve

For the mechanically minded, the Board of Governors of the Federal Reserve can be imagined as just that—a governor. For those of us with clean fingernails, a governor is a device installed on an engine to limit its horsepower after a certain point. Rented recreation vehicles like houseboats and go-carts have them to prevent injuries to equipment and person.

The Federal Reserve has interest rates. Or, specifically, the rate charged to banks by the Federal Reserve. That rate is usually reflected in short-term lending rates and then in all other rates downstream of it, from credit cards to savings accounts.

When it raises rates, the Fed wants to slow borrowing and spending. That keeps money on the sidelines (in savings) and hopefully keeps price inflation in check.

When the Fed lowers interest rates, it does it to spark borrowing and the spending of borrowed money, while discouraging savings. The aim is to create an environment where it's more advantageous to borrow money and spend it. If I'm saving for a new car and earning 2 percent, and then I can finance a car for just 3 percent, I'll probably head straight to the dealership. Money gets spent; the economy stays lively.

That's Fed 101. Now for the upper-level classes.

As this book was being written, the Fed kept cutting rates in order to spur growth. Sooner or later, and for a variety of reasons, the economy will return to expansion—and then the real stress on the Fed will become apparent.

As we've already defined in the Consumer Spending Progression, as a person approaches and then reaches retirement, he or she becomes practically allergic to debt. A sixty-six-year-old retiree on a tight budget simply isn't going to borrow a bunch of money no matter how low rates fall.

I often speak to large groups of people approaching retirement, or who are retired. I ask how many of them would borrow money at

5 percent, but the key is, you just can't borrow it and invest it, you have to borrow it and spend it. (That's what the Fed is trying to do, after all.) Out of 500 people, a few hands will go up. What if I dropped it to 3 percent? Maybe a few more think they'd borrow. One percent? A couple more. But what if I said money was free—literally 0 percent? Amazingly, no additional hands go up. It's simply not in their psychology of money to borrow, no matter how far rates fall. Ask a roomful of twenty- and thirty-year-olds the same questions, and you'd feel the breeze from so many hands waving: Pick me! Pick me!

So then, the Fed will be faced with the same basic set of monetary woes that Japan is facing now—a large population of debt-averse older people who won't borrow even though rates at Japanese banks are, as of this writing, effectively 0 percent.

The Fed-Chairman as Celebrity

Here's a question that most people can't answer: Who was the Fed Chairman before Alan Greenspan? I'll give you the answer at the end of the section, but the fact that most people don't know is quite telling.

In boom town America of the 1990s and into 2000, watching the stock markets was the nation's number one spectator sport. Entire cable networks and publishing empires were built to serve the insatiable demand for information. The Internet was seemingly designed for the obsessive stock watcher and questionable stock picker. Everyone watched Alan Greenspan as though he were Mick Jagger or Tom Cruise.

Mr. Greenspan has made some wise decisions, and some not-so-wise ones as well. But the most remarkable thing about his tenure is its timing. Alan Greenspan happened to be at the chairmen's desk during a time when 80 million baby boomers were making the most, spending the most, and investing the most. Not to take anything away from his accomplishments, but any reasonably intelligent economist could have probably done as well. Even the previous chairman, Paul Volker.

Private Pensions Under Stress

While traditional pension programs, or defined-benefit plans, have fallen out of fashion in corporate America (replaced by IRAs and 401[k] programs—defined *contribution* plans), there are still millions of baby boomers who have contributed to these programs and are expecting a payout. But there are stressors on the horizon.

First, the basics of a pension plan. It's a pool of assets, which assumes an interest rate it will earn and makes actuarial assessments on when you'll retire and how long you'll live after that. Based on those factors, a set dollar amount is put forth as a monthly or annual payout—the defined benefit. The problems start when interest rates and people refuse to play along.

Falling interest rates, fewer contributors, and healthier people bring significant stress to bear on these funds.

Who has pensions today? Many large manufacturing companies like automakers have pensions. State and municipal governments offer pensions to their employees. Police and fire departments and teachers all earn a pension. Some of the most deserving people in this country are at terrible risk of having their retirement savings devastated as pension funds come under what, for some, will be an unbearable weight.

Pension managers are greatly challenged to keep the fund balance high in low-rate environments. Consequently, they move the money to where it can earn more and stay fairly liquid. That means equities. And as long as equities can return a rate higher than the expected interest rate, everybody's happy.

But as boomers shift their wealth from growth to fixed income and leave the equity markets in a hurry (especially if volatility makes it an even more uncertain place), stock prices will almost certainly drop, if not dive. Not only are pension funds' returns falling, they may see substantial erosion in their principal as well. Add to that the people who were expected to live eight or ten years in retirement and instead live another thirty, and we may witness large pension funds in a crushing default.

Stress in the Banking System

At its core, banking is a simple business: there are depositors and there are borrowers. Banks increase or decrease the number of borrowers and depositors by increasing or decreasing interest rates. When rates go up, more depositors come in the door, and fewer borrowers. When rates go down, more borrowers and fewer lenders. Pretty basic stuff, and it's tended to keep banks on solid footing for fifty years or more. Banks have been able to keep the right balance, and thus return a consistent, if modest, profit to their shareholders.

Now, imagine a shift that dramatically reduces the number of borrowers, regardless of interest rates. Deposits will be high, as boomers move their money to government-protected, interest-bearing accounts. Indeed, banks will have piles of money in their vaults, but fewer opportunities to generate revenue off it.

It's hard to imagine bank failures on a large scale—the boomers will still need financial advice and will pay a fee to get it. And traditional borrowers won't disappear altogether. Traditional lending practices, however, may change radically. It's very easy to imagine a ruthlessly competitive environment to attract a smaller pool of borrowers. Credit card companies and on-line lenders will be smart and aggressive.

Low rates and intense competitive pressures will suppress profits. The weakest and slowest banks won't make it. The strongest and fastest will feel the stress.

When Stress Helps: Finding Good Opportunities in Bad News

Some positive effects will be seen as these various institutions deal with the changing environment. For example, low interest rates mean cheap money for first time homebuyers and all borrowers, be it on a credit card or a student loan.

In certain areas, thousands of boomer houses coming to market in a relatively short period is going to create a buyer's market. That and low mortgage rates, may deliver young families to their dream homes before the dream was even clear. Late-stage boomers who are still ten or fifteen years from retirement may be able to upgrade homes, or even finance a second home at rates far below their first.

Keep reading, because the rest of *Wealth Shift* is dedicated to helping you get on the right side of these negative trends, and profiting from them.

Stress in the State House and in City Hall

State and local governments have taxation authority over the homeowners, wage earners, and shoppers in their area. The money they raise through taxing income, property, and purchases is used to fund government at street level: public schools and hospitals, sewers and road repairs—all the infrastructure we call civilization.

State and local governments will be affected by the same forces we've discussed above: fewer high-wage earners and less overall spending. And that's if the boomers actually stick around town. If they leave, a new set of stresses emerge related to property.

Should the boomers continue the trends their parents have embraced, then northern and Midwestern cities may be facing a serious shortfall in property-tax revenues when property values flatten or decrease. When boomer homes flood the market, prices will erode, and property assessments will eventually reflect reduced property value. That means less property-tax revenue.

Clearly, some parts of the country will have the opposite problem—too many retirees exerting a different stress on the infrastructure. They may not be adding their share to the property-tax base because they rent or own a small condo. They almost certainly won't be bringing big purchases to the cash registers in town, so sales tax collections could lag. But every one of them will demand clean water and smooth roads.

We could even see areas with strong appeal to retirees transformed as retiree boomtowns, marked by dramatically climbing home prices and property taxes. Early boomer retirees and older folks might find themselves sitting on a gold mine—not a bad discovery at about the perfect time in life.

Even now, in 2003, Florida real estate in desirable areas is appreciating in the double digits, and sales activity in the real estate offices is increasing. One agent group in Naples has seen a 25 percent annual increase in the past three years.

The Consumer Economy Under Stress

We've talked about it throughout the book and will continue to do so. But a few points bear amplification here.

While its not a singular institution, the consumer economy as a whole is as important to this country's health as any other American institution mentioned in this chapter. To many other nations, it's the only American institution that matters.

The specific effect of the Wealth Shift on the consumer economy is difficult to predict right now, but a recession of some severity is a defensible guess. Perhaps a long and protracted recession. Perhaps a depression.

Japan's Wealth Shift is at the core of its recession that has, so far, resisted every treatment. And depression pressures are already mounting on the U.S. economy. The Great depression of the 1930s coincided with the retirement of a massive immigrant population. (Because it was the 1930s and conditions being what they were, retirees usually died a few years later, thus relieving the system of the burden. That won't happen again.) It also was marked by a time of determined and intentional geopolitical isolationism. The globalization of the 1920s stopped cold. Tariffs went up like walls around the country and effectively sealed our fate.

Today, global trade is deeply integrated into the consumer economy and there are thousands of multinational corporate structures that serve it. What could possibly dislodge them? The war on terrorism could possibly tighten more than security. Recent tariffs on steel imports are particularly worrisome. International transactions and international business in general could slow. Picture growth in promising markets stalled and expansion plans put on the shelf. Are these the ingredients for a depression? Not all of them, but they're a good start.

Chapter 3

Real Estate: Homeownership and Other Uncertain Investments

There's no ticker that runs along a property's baseboard with minute-by-minute updates on its value. That means profitable investing in real estate involves understanding the larger market swings and general trends. And it doesn't always even mean homeownership; winning investments in rental properties, homes for resale, commercial properties and real estate investment trusts (REITs) will be appearing during the Wealth Shift for both growth and income investors. In this chapter we'll talk about each, both in terms of the potential and the cautions.

Not surprisingly, the boomers have been driving housing trends since they bought their starter homes. During the Wealth Shift, they will remain a dominant force in housing, and their choices about where to live and what to buy will affect the value and profitability of commercial real estate.

What the boomers do as a natural and expected part of their lives will be creating numerous opportunities for all investors. Yet, not all investors will have real estate as a large part of their portfolios. Some won't have the patience. Some won't have the help. Some won't have the nerve.

But for investors with good timing, decent guidance, and at least a moderate taste for some good, old-school real estate speculation, the real estate upside could beat what the rest of the Wealth Shift markets have to offer.

Boomers as Housing Market Makers

The baby boomers have been holding the keys to the U.S. real estate market since the 1970s. That's when the boomers started buying their first homes, and it continued throughout the decade as wave after wave of twenty-something boomers started driving neighborhood streets, no longer looking for places to party or make out, but looking for homes to buy. As would be expected, those streets were the most crowded in the regions where the boomers had grown up—places where the U.S. population was also the most concentrated. Real estate agents will tell you that most first-time home buyers buy that home within fifty miles of their birthplace, and a full 70 percent of the baby boomers were born in the northeast regions of the U.S. or in California. Now look at the runup in housing prices in the northeast and the west coast during the 70s and early 80s. Home prices were increasing annually by double digits because of the increased demand and the lack of supply, and this despite soaring interest rates that should have put up barriers to homeownership. But the boomers needed homes and banks saw appreciating assets, so a lot of very expensive homes were purchased by a lot of young and optimistic Americans.

The homebuilder with a keen sense of demographics would have started building starter homes in about 1969. Instead, in order to accommodate this sudden "unexpected" demand, swarms of builders began swinging hammers by day and dreaming of huge margins by night. For many, that's exactly what happened. But the boomers have always had a way to drive supply past demand, and when those same homes were sold in the 1980s or early 1990s for prices equal or less than their decade-old valuation, it was clear just how diluted the market had become. There were still boomers buying homes, but they had kids now, and concerns about good schools, safe streets, and sensible commutes. It was time for other corners of the country to grow with the boomers.

Buying into the Heartland

The next ascent in home prices took place away from New York, Boston, and Los Angeles and occured in places like Denver, Atlanta, Minneapolis, St. Louis, Dallas/Ft. Worth, Seattle, and other regions where there was room to build and places to work. From 1988 to 2000, these places were the fastest-growing places in the nation, and housing prices rode right along with the boomers. Two factors were driving: one, the appeal of these places to new boomer families. Two, the presence of jobs as financial, technical, and other service-oriented businesses migrated away from the East, or were formed right here.

Which came first? Every business and every family has its own story, but the larger facts point to the presence of the right kind of workers as the tipping point in company relocation or formation. They'll always make cars in Detroit; that's where a mature infrastructure exists, from transportation to labor to automotive designers. But they'll also be making cars in Alabama and Tennessee, because that's where the car makers are finding the right kind of people to make the cars. Notice, too, that they are not building new factories in Minnesota, Maine, or, for that matter, Michigan.

Let me remind you once again that I'm using the language of demographics, not individual specifics. Obviously, every boomer did not flee the New York gridlock or the Los Angeles smog. But even the boomers who stayed close to home and started families of their own, made housing decisions based on their housing needs at the time, which brings us to the end of the history lesson, and into the forward looking part of the chapter.

Buyer's Market Ahead

Right now, America is well-stocked with 4,000 square feet, four-bedroom, four-bathroom, three-car-garage homes fifteen to twenty miles from the nearest city. Its what the boomers built to raise their kids, and plenty of boomers are right in the middle of that life phase now. Remember, the youngest baby boomers are in their early forties as this is being written. They still need those bedrooms, bathrooms, and playrooms. But the largest group of baby boomers, those born between 1948 and 1955, are already starting to look around half-empty homes and ask, "What's next?" But the real question should actually be, "Who's next?"

Who will buy the millions of "McMansions" that ring the cities of St. Louis, Indianapolis, Chicago, Detroit, and many other places? Those late-stage boomers still need bigger homes, and low interest rates are helping keep housing prices strong in those areas—for now, in 2003. Soon, the demographic wave will break, and the market will be flooded with these homes. It's going to be a fantastic market for homebuyers because, elemental economics, they will be scarce.

Buyers of those homes will be few because the population of people who need such homes will be in a trough. Some late-stage boomers will move up, and some Gen-Xers will be ready to move their families in, but the next significant group of buyers for these homes are the kids who grew up in them—the echo boomers—and they are still finishing college, establishing their careers, and buying starter homes—the 2,200 square foot, three-bedroom, two-bath, two-car-garage homes that are popping up where corn and soybeans were growing just last summer.

Homeownership in the Wealth Shift

The baby boomers are and will be, quite naturally, moving into homes that match their needs. If you are an early or mid-stage boomer, somewhere in your early to mid-fifties, and living in a home with lots of family appeal, move now. If you're a late-stage boomer, with kids packed into a home that's feeling smaller by the day, try to hold out a few more years. You know those big houses you're looking at longingly today? Soon, their owners will be looking at you the very same way.

So here's the essential question: What's the right home to have now? Answer: the ones the boomers are going to want as they move into retirement, and fully retire.

Let's look at those homes—where they are, and what they mean to investors.

Go South, Old Man

The current housing trends in warm-weather areas like Florida, Phoenix, the Gulf Coast, the southeastern United States and Las Vegas offers investors a no-brainer lesson in retirement lifestyles: Old folks dislike the cold.

Does that mean that every retiring boomer is destined for these places? Enough are so as to make homeownership in these areas and others with friendly winter climates a sharp investment right now, or in the very near future. If you're close to retirement, and know where you want to move, buy now—even if it means downsizing here while you wrap up parenting and your careers. In 2003, I'm advising people to get a stake in their future retirement neighborhood early. They might not end up living in that exact home, but they will have an asset that's appreciating right along with homes in the area they already want to buy in.

And if it means unloading that big suburban palace a few years before they planned, do it anyway. Large changes are inevitable: they *will* retire, they *will* move, they *will* get old. May as well be steering the process versus merely trying to hang on as it begins to careen.

Get Smaller, Safer, and Have Plenty of Room for Cocktails

The homes the boomers will want to live in during their most active retirement years will be homes that are easy to maintain, easy to get around in, and offer more room for entertaining. Staircases will be out. Ranches with open floor plans will be in. The boomers in early retirement won't be moving as fast as they were when chasing kids and building careers, but they won't be pushing walkers either. They will be active and social, just like now, without all the kids running around.

And while these homes in warmer, southern regions will be of a particular premium, the boomer demographic is large enough to put a premium on just about any home that meets their needs in retirement. The boomers are all aging at the same rate, regardless of their income or social standing. Many will be looking for homes in Naples. Many will be looking in State College, Pennsylvania, too.

In fact, there is a housing trend just under way in many larger college towns. Boomers and other older, now retired alumni are moving to town to live. And why not? There's lots of good memories, plenty of volunteer and educational opportunities, and a world of cultural and athletic events to keep the active retiree on the go. Compared to another ice cream social at some Florida country club, university events are positively invigorating.

Returning to Downtown with Symphony Season Tickets in Hand

Cultural stimulation will be a priority for a large portion of the newly retired boomers. Driving in from the suburbs, however, will not. Already, in cities with established urban living and in those where homes, apartments, and condos are just now starting to arrive in significant numbers, older boomers and folks just ahead of them on the demographic scale are living right next door to the affluent singles and childless professional couples who traditionally live in these kinds of dwellings.

Once again, if this is the kind of lifestyle that appeals to you in retirement, and you're within ten years or so of retiring, buy there now. There's going to be a reverse migration back downtown when the first of seventy-plus million boomers begin to buy homes that fit with their newfound freedom.

Health Care Infrastructures: Some States Will Do Better

For many of the baby boomers, retirement will come at a time when the largest questions will not be where to tee off from but how to pay for the golf and everything else that comes with living without a job. The wildcard for millions will be health care.

As discussed in earlier chapters, the pensions that included generous health care coverage will be largely absent from most boomer's retirement. (Even their parents, who have pensions, are now battling with their former companies over the retraction of benefits.) Boomers will probably need to pick up the tab on their health care insurance until Medicare kicks in at sixty-five. That means millions of retired boomers could go for five years or more with a significant insurance bill of $1,500 or more to pick up each month. They could also get some unlikely help from their statehouse.

Some states have created pools that help retirees share the risk of insurance and keep rates lower, and once people start doing the research and the math, there could be a lot of other states looking into ways to keep retirees inside their borders, or to attract boomers to their states. Alabama isn't Florida, but if they can pass laws that hold insurance rates down in comparison, they'll get their share of retirees, which could number in the hundreds of thousands, if not more.

It's something to consider as you make decisions about when

to sell and what to buy. Health and health care will only intensify as issues of importance to boomers. These issues will intersect every aspect of their lives, from where they live to the kinds of homes they live in. As an investor, and as a homeowner, you must understand the power these boomers have to move housing markets their way.

Rental Properties and Homes for Resale: Location, Location, Location

Some investors already have integrated real estate into their portfolios. They may have been buying and selling property—usually homes for rental and resale—for as long as they've been investing. Others are new to the game, but thrilled by the potential gains in comparison to tepid returns in equities. The old real estate wisdom is true: They aren't making any more of it.' "They" also aren't guaranteeing the returns on the real estate you happen to buy, so let's look at a few common-sense strategies for buying and selling homes, and even apartment buildings, before and during the Wealth Shift.

Starting with homes for resale, the underlying principle is the same for your principle residence: Buy the property that someone else is going to pay more for later. And like every other piece of advice in this book, demographics are the starting point. Before you pick up the real estate section or call your favorite agent, arm yourself with a good understanding of the two demographic groups who will be buying most of the homes in the run up to the Wealth Shift, and inside it proper.

They are echo boomers buying their first or second home. And they are boomers buying a home to retire in. Let's look at the first group.

Echo boomers will be looking for homes that fit singles, couples, and young families. They will want to be close to the action: restaurants, recreation, their workplaces, and their friends. Think bungalows and smaller, older suburban homes. Those four-bedroom/four-baths way out there past the mall won't make their list, and as we've already discussed, buyers for those homes may be in short supply for a long, long time. Echo boomers aren't going to be showing the same bias toward warmer climes, so if you're in the Midwest or East, or even the North and find a few perfect homes for echo boomers on their way up, think about signing the mortgage. Money will be cheap for you and your prospective buyers, and new mortgage programs that let young buyers start early are helping close a lot of deals that would not have happened ten years earlier.

On to the boomers, and the homes they'll want. Everything that I've presented up until now holds true here too: Boomers will be going for smaller places with more room to entertain, less yard to mow, and increased access to cultural institutions. Of course, sometimes, a quiet pond passes for culture, which brings me to another kind of home to look for in anticipation of boomer buyers.

Remember, not every boomer is going south, but they are all going to go somewhere, and plenty are going to want to stay close to their kids and grandkids. So think about those places an hour or so outside the city, maybe a small lake or a small town. Peaceful, quiet, and close. Every area and each home is an individual case, but don't rule them out before you take a look and put yourself in a retiring boomer's sensible shoes.

Last category for rentals: multiunit properties. These will almost exclusively be for echo boomers and younger, and the same cheap financing that might make these properties affordable are also creating opportunities for your renters to buy and move out. At the same time, there will probably always be a market for good, safe, well-maintained apartments as long as they are close to work and play. These deals are probably limited partnerships versus principle ownership. So that partnership deal is key to your success. Hint: get a good contract attorney.

And before you get involved in one of these deals, study the vacancy rates in the area, read the census data on numbers of potential renters, and pay close attention to where other renters are working. Apartment owners with the right properties and the right instincts can use both to generate a strong cash flow and set the table for a profitable sale. Easy? Rarely. But the Wealth Shift will keep everyone lively on their toes; some of you might just find that multiunit properties are as good a place, or better, to be doing your investment dance.

☛ *Resales and Rentals During the Wealth Shift*

Think about boomers and echo boomers, and no one else. Buy, or invest in, what they will want to live in. It's about the property type and the location. Use the low interest rates to increase your buying power, but be prepared to lose renters as those same low rates turn them into homeowners. You won't have to be buying homes on the Florida beach to make money here—buy 'em if you're lucky enough to find them—but there will be boomer buyers in *every* state. Think ahead, and you might get ahead.

Commercial Properties: Opportunities Covered in Plywood

I don't want to spend a lot of time on commercial real estate. It's risky, complex, and tough, even for the pros. But even everyday investors may find profitable investments in this sector if they can bring some demographic awareness to bear.

It starts with knowing where the boomers are going to want to live in retirement. They won't just be living in that area, they'll be shopping, and going to the hair salon, and dinner, too (before 6:00 p.m., of course). Commercial property that is undervalued for present market conditions might be ready to jump quickly once boomers begin to live nearby. Read that last sentence and emphasize the *"might."* Many a buyer has waited for the payday phone call that never came. But property has a welcome habit of appreciating, and for some parcels, it's going to happen in a hurry once the boomers start their retirement and investors everywhere absorb the impact their buying habits are having on the economy.

Final note on these purchases: Limited partnerships are common, and a good way to spread the risk. But keep that attorney's number close.

REITs: Income and Growth, Maybe

REITs were created by Congress in 1961 as a way for individual investors to own commercial real estate while preserving liquidity. To qualify, a company must pay at least 90 percent of its taxable income to shareholders each year. The REITs earn a nice tax break, and shareholders can earn more dividend income.

REITs are usually specialists in very specific type of properties-shopping malls, Class-A high rises, nursing homes, apartments, hotels, self-storage facilities. You name the commercial real estate category, and there is a REIT investing in those properties.

While REITs are sensitive to rate fluctuations in whatever way the specific properties are sensitive to them, they are much more of a barometer to consumer and business demand. The soft economy and terrorist attacks of 2001 hurt REITs invested in lodging and resort properties—they were down over 15 percent. At the same time, hospital and health care soared over forty percent.

These investments perform well when they can keep occupancy and rents high, and when they can bring new properties into the trust. Essentially, it's a cash flow business, which is a good thing for income or growth investors as long as they are invested in the right REIT.

☞ *REITs During the Wealth Shift*

Look for REITs that specialize in health care, nursing homes, retirement communities, and anything related to retirement and an aging population. Even resorts are expected to return to the positive side as the retired boomers hit the road. REITs that have a geographic focus, like the southwest and Florida, could be attractive to an income investor. Stay away from REITs that engage in commercial real estate in the Midwest. High vacancy rates will hold those returns down.

Chapter 4
Investing for Income:
The Environment, the Instruments, and the Strategies

Moving from growth to income investing is a natural part of the Consumer Spending Progression presented in Chapter 1. We get older. We stop working for our income. Our investments generate the income. But even in a calm economic environment, it's not always an easy transition. Embracing an income mindset is hard for many growth investors who have never understood bonds and have never even seen a dividend check. In the low interest-rate environment of the Wealth Shift, income generation will challenge every investor, every advisor, and every financial institution.

In This Chapter

First, we'll take a macro view of the landscape as the boomers near and then enter retirement. That's essentially their starting point as income investors. Then we'll move quickly into some of the specific tools available for income investors, with bonds at the center. It's not an all-inclusive tour of any of the available choices; each category deserves its own book, and I urge you to keep reading, and keep talking to your advisor about your own retirement planning.

What you *will* find here are predictions and cautions about how each income investment instrument will perform up to and during the coming Wealth Shift.

Then, we'll tie it all together by aggregating the instruments into

distinct planning strategies designed for different investors and vary-
ing portfolios.

The Environment: A Historical Precedent

The baby boomers will enter retirement in a way no other generation has before.

They will be healthier.
Retirement for the WWII generation and all previous genera-
tions was a time of diminished health and generally limited longevity.
The baby boomers will be healthier and their life expectancy longer.
That means twenty, thirty, or even forty years of retired living.

They will be on their own.
The two structures that previously supported retirees have virtually vanished in America. Traditional pensions are few and the extended family has disappeared. Boomers will be relying almost
exclusively on capital assets created during their working lives—
their savings, real estate, 401(k)s, IRAs, and SEPs—to support
them in their retirement. And while the kids may have moved home
for a few years after college, don't expect them to willingly throw
open the door once their parents start to struggle. An extended family under one roof is rare in this country. But that, too, could be
changing.

They won't be counting on Social Security.
Even a solvent Social Security Administration won't be offering
this generation the income they need to live in the way they expect
to. The American concept of retirement has changed from a time of
retreat, recovery, and rest to a period of personal expansion: travel
entertainment . . . hobbies, all from a well-appointed home in a very
desirable location. It's no surprise that a monthly Social Security

check just isn't going to buy the boomers the kind of retirement they expect.

There will be so many of them.

Just as they shaped the markets of their youth and middle age, the boomers will shape the markets of their retirement and near-retirement years. Income instruments of the Wealth Shift could be the minivans of the 80s—there won't be enough of them and they'll be priced accordingly. But unlike minivans, income investment instruments can't simply be manufactured to meet growing demands, and although those overpriced minivans drove just fine, when the price goes up on an income investment the effective yield goes down.

Same Tool, Different Rules

The financial tools for generating investment income will change very little in structure once the Wealth Shift occurs. People will continue to rely on short-term instruments (like CDs and money markets), mortgage funds, bonds, and REITs. What will change is the potential of those tools to deliver a fixed return you can live on . . . and on and on and on for twenty or thirty years or more.

All traditional fixed-income investments are tied to capital markets in essentially the same way: borrowers are issuing debt—or borrowing money; lenders are lending the money, and then guaranteeing a fixed rate of return. The problems during the Wealth Shift will arise when two key factors are disrupted. One is interest rates and the other is supply.

Low Rates: Low Income

As boomers became growth investors in the 1990s, we saw equity markets surge as never before. The economy boiled, and the Fed kept rates high to manage the heat. Yet when 70 million boomers begin to change from borrowers and growth investors to savers and income investors, interest rates could be dropping quickly, or already be close to zero. They'll stay low, too. The early-stage baby boomers (and even younger ones looking ahead) will want to lend, not borrow—they want somebody else using their money and paying them interest. Which means rates will remain suppressed, since demand is flat or declining.

What's the impact of all these savers on the rest of us? If you have a million dollars dedicated to income and can only find a 2 percent CD, your million bucks is producing only $20,000 a year. That's not much of an income for a big balance, and most will have much less.

Fewer New Issues: Fewer Income Opportunities

As *Wealth Shift* was being written, a trend in fixed income securities was continuing: there were fewer and fewer of them being issued. Essentially, governments and corporations are, like the aging boomers, becoming debt-averse. They are not asking for money, either, because they don't need it or because they don't want the liability on their books (what will Wall Street think of all that debt?)

It's a trend that will almost certainly continue; in fact it will probably get worse. For example, there won't be nearly the same number of mortgages to invest in once the boomers pay off their mortgages altogether, or refinance their loans to increasingly lower rates.

In October of 2001, the U.S. government stopped issuing thirty-year debt. This is a clear sign that they no longer need the long-term financing or they, too, see low rates ahead and don't want to lock into today's higher rates for a three-decade payout. Either way, new thirty-year treasuries are no longer on the investment income menu.

Moving Away from Equities Now, in the Early 2000s

A shift is happening right now. There is a recognizable movement away from equities and toward fixed income.

The market volatility of 2000 and 2001 has driven millions of boomers and their investment advisors to look at bonds and other more stable investments (a.k.a. income) with fresh eyes. The U.S. bond market is as strong as it's been in a decade. Aside from the fact that bonds typically do well when stocks don't, bonds are also a comforting introduction to fixed-income investing around the time when many boomers are watching their retirement calendars.

It's going to be a tough decision to move that money back out into the uncertain waters of the equity markets after it's been in the calm, safe harbors of fixed income. Some of that money will stay there, which means there will be even less new debt available to invest in once the full-scale shift occurs and the boomers start retiring en masse.

Bonds are even earning their place on the TV tickers. CNBC has started putting the ten-year Treasury Note ticker at the bottom. There's the S&P, NASDAQ, Dow, and the ten-year note plus occasionally the five-year note. Now imagine a time when viewers can see at a glance the thirty-, twenty-, and ten-year bond-corporate debts, high-grade, low-grade, and, at the bottom of the stack, the Dow. The financial media respond to what investors are interested in, and in the Wealth Shift, they're going to become interested in interest.

Getting into bonds early could look like a very smart decision, but you could also get there too early and miss out on the last equity bull market that boomers will ride.

Timing Is Everything, Here's the Starting Line

Let's look at the calendar and make some safe predictions. Then, we'll examine specific categories of income investments and their inherent risks.

The first boomers start retiring in 2008 when they turn sixty-two. So in 2008, you're going to see significant pressure to buy income investments. That's when the gold rush begins. New retirees and near-retirees are going to be looking for those little nuggets of high-yield income investments. And those are going to become more rare, meaning yields will be down. But what about before 2008?

I think the period between 2003 and 2008 will be a good time to be in equities. A strengthening economy will keep corporate revenues moving upward and taking rates along with them as the Fed reacts to keep expansion (read inflation) in check. It could well be the final bull market in equities of the boomers' growth investing. So in addition to getting in on what equity growth the market presents, that will be the time to start to capture your income investments, especially if you see retirement ahead in four to seven years. High or rising rates will always attract sharp bond buyers aiming to capture higher yields before rates inevitably fall again. Be one of them.

This middle part of the decade could be a great time to lock in a rate around five percent or six percent, or even seven percent, because your twenty-year Treasury bond at six percent is going to be very marketable if interest rates drop to three, or two, or even one percent. That's a good income, an appreciating asset, and a safe harbor all in one.

If you're going to retire ten to fifteen years down the road, go to the growth chapter where you'll find strategies that also include bonds, just not in the same concentration. If you're retired, or can see it approaching on the near horizon, keep reading.

Steady Principal or Steady Income? Pick One

When investors' tolerance for risk is low, they tend to think exclusively about preserving their principal value. But there's another way of thinking that's closer to what these investors really want. Because very risk-averse investors are, by default, investing for income, they would do better to think about preserving a steady income versus keeping their principal absolutely unchanged.

If you insist on a principal that is in absolutely no risk and cannot diminish, go buy a short-term CD or put your cash in a money market, and sleep well knowing that every cent will be there when you wake up. What might have changed, however, is the income you're earning from it. In 2000 and 2001, rates moved from 7.5 percent down to two percent. An income investor earning those rates off a million-dollar principal just saw their income go from $75,000 to $20,000. As you're reading this, the rates could well be back up to five percent or higher. Suddenly your rock-solid investment is starting to look uncertain, if not downright skittish. These instruments are fine for preservation alone but are uncertain generators of income—which should be the income investor's primary concern. Let's keep shopping.

Here's a twenty-year bond, and let's say interest rates are 5.5 percent. If you have $100,000 invested here, you know your income stream is going to be $5,500 a year every year for the remaining maturity. No matter what happens to rates, you've locked in a level of income performance. But rates do matter to you, because if you need to sell that bond any time before maturity, its value is going to depend upon where interest rates are and the bond market's reaction to them. When you go to sell, those bonds could be worth less than you paid. Such is the cost of a steady income stream, but one worth careful consideration for the income investor.

The Unsettling Presence of Risk in Income Investing

Income investors will be facing the very real condition of reinvestment risk: This is the risk inherent in finding a new investment at the point where the previous vehicle retires, matures, or is sold. It's when your money loses the roof over its head and has to look (or scramble) for a new place to live.

For example, you might have a one-year CD at six percent but at the end of that year, you get your money back and you have to reinvest it. Your investment options at that moment are the reinvestment risk you face, which you essentially agreed to when you bought the CD a year ago.

It may look tame compared to the typical risks in equities, but for the investor living on that income, reinvestment risk matters very much. In fact, it has the power to change the very definition of safety. Because these traditionally "safe" investments like CDs (which merely promise a set return at a future point in time) also carry substantial reinvestment risks, and those risks jeopardize the monthly income, then they really aren't as safe as many have imagined. They may even be risky.

Not to worry—in the following sections of this chapter, we'll be looking at the advantages and disadvantages of individual investment instruments, and putting them into the context of the approaching Wealth Shift.

What About Inflation? Heck, What About Deflation?

Income investors have always faced inflation as a risk. You get a $100,000 bond today at 6.5 percent and earn $6,500. It's a particular issue for investors who are going to live twenty or thirty years on income from bonds and other traditional income investments. Problem is, the Wealth Shift may actually create a deflationary environment.

In other words, you've got too few dollars chasing too many goods. Efficiencies in production and distribution of goods may surge ahead of the demand. As we established in the

Consumer Spending Progression, retired boomers simply aren't going to be buying a lot of new computers, new cars, or new homes.

The good news for investors in deflationary times is that earning low interest rates isn't all that bad because the growth in the value of the asset relative to the purchase of goods has increased. If you can keep the value of your principal steady during deflationary times, the cost of goods is getting cheaper— your dollars buy more, even if you may not be earning more of them.

The Instruments

Bonds: Essential Tools for Income Investors

First, an introduction to the mechanics of a bond, then a broad overview of the many different types and, along the way, what to look for (and be wary of) as the boomers drag us all into the Wealth Shift. First a few key terms.

Maturity Date

Bonds are bought two ways: at issuance, and on the open market. Every bond has a hard maturity date. On that day, the bondholder gets the par value back (the original issue price, in other words), regardless of whether they were the original investor. A bond may be bought and sold a hundred times in the twenty years it takes to mature.

Call Features

A "call" is a component included in many bonds that allows the issuer to take back the bond and pay you back before it matures. Some bonds have long calls, or call dates close to the maturity, and others have shorter calls. Income investors in low-interest-rate environments are wise to be aware, even wary, of calls. Here's why:

Say a corporation issues a debt for ten years and they're paying 12 percent. That bond is going to attract a lot of income investors' money. But it has a call feature that says four years down the road, they can pay you back. Then rates go down, and the 12 percent return you were counting on for the next fifteen years vanishes when the corporation is able to refinance the debt at the lower rate. Happens all the time. They may have to pay you a small premium to give you back your money sooner, but that hardly compensates income investors for the reinvestment risk they are suddenly facing when a bond is called. In the Wealth Shift, calls will happen even more frequently as low rates encourage refinancing of new debt to even lower rates in interest.

Calls also get to a basic reality of bonds: they are a debt that the debtors are anxious to get rid of as soon as possible. Bond holders are not stockholders, and bond issuers—especially corporations—are not keeping your best interests in mind any more that you are keeping MasterCard's best interests in mind when you examine that bill each month. The sooner that balance is down to $0, the better.

Coupon

This is your payday voucher. A coupon is the part of a bond that denotes the amount of interest due and on what date and where the payment is to be made. Bearer coupons are presented to the issuer's designated paying agent or deposited in a commercial bank for collection. A coupon can also be registered, which means the interest payment is mailed directly to the registered holder. Coupons are generally payable semiannually.

Four essential facts

1. Bonds are finite. Bonds exist only to the same degree as a need to borrow capital exists. In other words, if a government or corporation doesn't need the money, they're not about to borrow it just to keep the bond market supplied with product. It's a classic supply-and-demand scenario. And when the supply side of the dynamic is slow to produce, the demand will inevitably rise, and with it, price.

2. The bond market sets prices that limit effective bond yields, and it is an extremely effective market. Bond prices are set by the bond desks of the big traders and brokerages—houses that own hundreds of millions of bonds and broker even more for their bond clients. If these guys won't give you $1,300 for your $1,000 bond paying 6 percent, then no one will. Bond traders use their considerable muscle to hold the value of all bonds for sale roughly equal to what new issues are paying at that time, or roughly equal to the current rates.

Here's a simple example. Let's say you own that $1,000 bond at 6 percent. It matures in twenty years. That's an easy $60 per year for the next twenty years. Now, you want to place that same bond on the market to see what it might fetch. Well, the first question is what are interest rates doing right now? Three percent. Okay, that means your 6 percent bond looks pretty sweet, the bond market agrees and sets the price at $1,300. Why not more or less? Because they do the math.

That $1,300 price means the effective yield is just 4.6 percent, or $60 a year. Then there's the loss when the bond matures. Remember, it's a loan, so whoever is holding the bond at the time of maturity gets the original amount back—in this case $1,000—$300—less than you paid twenty years ago. That's the depreciation, and when it's spread over two decades it drops the effective yield on your bond paying 4.6 percent another 1.5 percent. Look at that: the six percent bond is delivering an effective yield of about three percent—just what the rest of the market is paying. And this happens again and again, in thousands of transactions a day—a very efficient market, indeed.

3. The volatility in bond prices is more pronounced with longer maturities. When a bond is ten, fifteen, or twenty years from maturity, there will be more price volatility because there is more uncertainty in long-term rates. Price fluctuates along a larger range, reflecting this uncertainty. At two or three years to maturity, more is known about the interest rate environment, so the appreciating or depreciating value can be more accurately predicted. Thus, prices move along a tighter range.

4. Rising interest rates will reduce the value of bonds on the market. Falling rates will increase their market value. The bonds with the longest maturity dates are the ones most affected by movements up or down the interest rate continuum. In other words, small interest rate decreases will raise the value of short-term bonds slightly, but long-term bonds will show a significant rise in value. Bottom line: when rates are ticking up, its better to be holding short-term bonds; when they're ticking down, long-term bonds are better.

Bonds and bond trading are complexity defined. It's an intricate and sophisticated market, and I've merely offered a quick peek in the door. It's said that the smartest guys on Wall Street are running the bond desks. So getting help from an advisor with experience in bonds is Job One for the income investor, especially during the Wealth Shift when demand will be high, supply will be low as less debt is issued, and rates will be bringing effective yields down to earth—all aided by the cold efficiency of the bond market.

Basic Types of Bonds

Bonds are the foundation of an income investment portfolio. That's going to be true before the Wealth Shift begins, as well as after. Buying the right bonds has never been easy. During the depressed rate environment that's looming, income investors and their bond advisors will have to be even smarter. Here's a quick look at the instruments and what the Wealth Shift may bring. (And when I say quick, I mean it. There are hundreds, if not thousands of bonds on the market, each with different structures, features, and risks. If you know bonds, you know how complicated the menu is. If you don't, start here. Then take the information specific to the Wealth Shift with you as you learn more.)

And remember, regardless of the bond type, income-hungry boomers are going to want them. So buy them first. Lock in your yield before the flood of buyers raises prices and lowers effective yields.

Treasuries

Debt issued by the federal government is rock-solid safe, especially the longer term bonds with limited calls that greatly reduce reinvestment risk. For income investors during good economic times with higher rates, treasury bonds are a a quality debt.

☛ *Treasuries During the Wealth Shift*

Before and during the Wealth Shift, treasury bonds could be very attractive to all investors, including those more interested in appreciating wealth than in generating income. But I'll say it again: buy them first. Lock in those rates—and not for one or two or three years, that's too much exposure to reinvestment risk in a low-rate environment that could last a decade. Lock them in for fifteen or twenty years, and be ready to buy when rates rise just prior to 2007–2009.

Municipal

Municipal bonds come in an endless variety, with choices along the complete safety continuum. The two most common are general obligation (G.O.) bonds and revenue bonds—that's the debt issued to raise money for stadiums, libraries, and schools.

Municipal bonds have one very appealing feature to income investors: in most cases, interest income is not taxed. There are exception (AMT bonds, for example), but in the majority of cases, no taxes are owed on the interest the bondholder is paid, no matter what tax bracket or tax situation the holder may be in. However, if the bond appreciates and is sold at a profit, you'll have to give the revenuers their due.

☛ *Municipals and the Wealth Shift*

As with treasuries, go for long maturities. And buy them in diverse locations with a bias to the south. States in the northern part of the country are going to be facing some real challenges keeping their budgets in balance. Could their bonds default? You bet. Declining tax revenues as the boomers stop spending, stop owning, or move South will put some Northern and Midwestern communities between the proverbial rock and a hard spot. The boomers will be the rock. The weakened economy will be the hard spot.

Corporate

In the corporate bond environment, income investors will find a veritable salad bar of bond choices with risks and rewards to match. There are companies nearly as rock-solid as the government—think GE. Those companies issue what's called investment-grade bonds. And then there are the other kinds, with Moody's and Standard & Poor's ratings from AAA to D. Corporate bonds with a B rating and below are called high-yield, also called noninvestment grade or "junk bonds."

In junk bonds, you'll encounter a higher degree of risk and a higher potential yield than with other bonds. They are often associated with companies who are struggling with multiple negative pressures, such as excessive leveraging, corporate takeovers, and leveraged buyouts.

D means default. (But there is always potential for these companies to recover, and investors line up to grab corporates at 5¢ on the dollar, betting on a recovery and dreaming of a big payday.)

☛ *Corporates During the Wealth Shift*

During the Wealth Shift, it's very likely that these corporate debts, especially the junk, will come under considerable stress. At the same time, corporate debt issuance could emerge as the capital-of-choice as this decade progresses. Yes, even the junk. Imagine a minefield with oil underneath. Here are three things to know about corporates as we enter the Wealth Shift:

1. THE WEALTH SHIFT WILL WEAKEN (OR TOPPLE) WEAK COMPANIES

Because a corporate bond relies on the revenue generated by a corporation, the bond is only as safe as the corporation is successful at generating revenue. Thus, in good economic times and in bad, there will always be corporations that default. Now, imagine the pressure all companies will face as consumer spending slows and economic activity drops to recession levels or worse. When a corporation defaults on its debts, the money's all gone. There's no income, there's no principal, and there's no government to bail them out with raised taxes or new money supply. Yet, like almost everything else happening during the Wealth Shift, opportunities are created as well.

2. BAD DEBTS CAN CREATE SWEET OPPORTUNITIES

When some corporate debt defaults, the entire low-grade corporate bond market softens and exposes great debt opportunities with good companies. Case in point: telecommunications debt and defaults in 2000.

When those companies went down, the entire corporate bond market dropped. It didn't matter whether you were in telecom or not. The whole corporate bond market fell apart, and sharp investors were picking up debt that was qualified as junk debt, but from companies that were not as much at risk. Some of that debt was paying fifteen percent or even twenty percent based on bond prices at the time. How did that happen? Say a bond was paying nine percent, or $90 a year on a $1,000 investment, and in a soft bond market that same bond is trading for thirty cents on the dollar. Buy it, and you're paying $300 to get the $90 in income, or a twenty-seven percent yield—a good move in a bad market, assuming that you could tolerate the risks that are inherent with corporate bonds. While treasuries and municipals are traded on interest rates alone, corporate exist in a world much closer to stocks, and that's a place where economic and business issues come into play more directly.

So economic slowdowns and even calamity can create opportunity in the corporate environment. The key is good timing, good advice, and enough diversity to protect you when the environment inevitably changes again.

3. THE SAFEST BONDS MAY HAVE THE SHORTEST CALLS

Not surprisingly, the safest corporate debt is issued by the largest and most stable companies. They are also the companies that tend to issue debt with prominent call features. Well-run companies are eager to discharge their debts as soon as they can. In the debt-averse environment of the Wealth Shift, these calls will get even shorter. Which means that these highly rated bonds carry a clear reinvestment risk for income investors. Ironically, the companies are so strong that you can't count on them to generate income for the long haul.

BEATING THE BABY BOOMERS TO BONDS

In an economic downturn or worse, the equities markets aren't the most viable way for a corporation to raise money. During the Wealth Shift, we may see companies issuing debt over equity. In fact, it's already happening: 2001 saw several major debt issuances by blue-chip corporations like GM and others.

And why not? Interest rates are staying low, and it's a good borrowing environment for everyone. What's more, there are lots of growth investors out there who are seeing too many negatives on their portfolio statements and are moving to bonds for better return. Add in twenty or thirty million fifty-something boomers thinking about income over growth, and the bond market will get very hot.

So you want to own them before the rest of the boomers want them. Look at the opportunity even if you're five or six years out from retirement; start to lock in high rates. After 2007 or so, there may be virtually no bonds on the market that offer effective yields comparable with yields available now, in the early 2000s. And if your time horizon is short, or you are in retirement and investing for income now, start buying now.

As with so many other investments, the key is timing and getting the right advice. That means enlisting the help of a savvy and seasoned bond advisor who also recognizes the demographic shift taking place. These are complicated instruments and your income is too important. You may have made some good guesses in stocks (who didn't during the bull-run) but don't push your luck in bonds.

Bond Funds

Sharing risk and reward is as common in bonds as it is with stocks and mutual funds—with just as many varieties of products and sellers. Here are two major categories of funds, with their attendant risks and potential rewards defined in basic terms. One has a lot of growth potential to offer income investors during the Wealth Shift. The other offers mostly uncertainty.

Open-End Bond Funds

An open-end bond mutual fund operates like an open-end stock mutual fund—investors can come and go as they please. Which means that timing is essential for a successful income investor.

Let's say you're the first one in the door at the XYZ Bond Fund, and the fund manager takes your money and buys an 8 percent bond. Is this fund manager happy to just sit there with you, holding your hand while the income streams your way? Certainly not. XYZ wants more investors in the fund, and they use the 8 percent they're earning for you as an incentive to new investors. So here comes a bunch of new investors looking for eight percent, which is fine when rates are steady or rising. But what if they are falling? The fund manager still takes the new money out into the environment and buys new bonds, which are now paying seven percent. Now your yield is going down because you're pooled with all these other investors.

The very same fund manager would interrupt me here and say that these funds are long-term vehicles with long-term strategies that deliver consistent income while pooling the risk. Sure. In normal economic cycles this is true, but during the Wealth Shift when income investors will outnumber all others, open-end bond funds are going to be attracting more and more money. All the while, rates are likely to be falling lower and lower. The first guys in earned comparatively high rates, but everyone who buys in later gets a piece of it.

☞ *Open-End Bond Funds During the Wealth Shift*

Be skeptical. Unless they are joining the fund late in the game, or simply feeling generous to people you will never know, income investors will be wise to keep most of their money out of open-end bond funds—many millions will be knocking on the door, and you just never know the kinds of people they'll let in.

Closed-End Bond Funds

In a closed-end bond fund, an Initial Public Offering is issued to attract a pool of money. The fund manager takes that money into the bond environment and buys the bonds consistent with the advertised strategy. Then they close the door. If you're in, you're in. And if you're out, you can still get in, but without diluting the original investment of the people already in.

That's because the fund also issues stock in the fund just like a corporation would, and these portions of equity in the bond fund can be traded exactly like any other stock. Investors don't really own the bonds anymore; they own stock in how the bonds are performing.

And unlike the long maturities of the bonds held by the fund, the stocks are completely liquid. Every closed end fund has a Net Asset Value (N.A.V.), which is simply the total value of the fund divided by the number of shares issued. That number moves as the value of the portfolio moves, but capital markets set the actual price for the shares.

Institutional investors and brokers, as well as studious individual investors, consider factors like the track record of the fund manager. A hot manager who can deliver higher yields naturally attracts more buyers, and the market then sets a premium price for the shares.

Shares in the fund might be worth $10 based solely on the N.A.V., but the market may have set the price $9.50. That means the shares are trading at a discount. If the fund's per-share price on the market is higher than the N.A.V., the market has set a premium price. Not surprisingly, closed end funds priced at a discount can have the greatest appeal to buyers.

And if you see volatility here, you're right, but who cares? Remember, income investors have the choice of principal preservation or income generation, but not both. In this case, the price of a high income is principal volatility. The key is timing and good advice, which gets you into a closed-end fund at a discount price. Then, you're set to capture whatever appreciation occurs while you keep your income flowing.

☞ *Closed-End Bond Funds During the Wealth Shift*

These funds have a clear appeal to income investors because the fund manager isn't going to be forced to take new money and find new bonds. He or she has a pool of funds earning interest and paying dividends. These dividends pay the fund's expenses and a consistent income for you. Plus immediate liquidity. Plus a well-managed instrument. If you can't tell already, I like closed-end funds for income investors. And I expect to recommend them even more as the boomers start driving the Wealth Shift.

Bond Funds: Leveraged or Unleveraged?

This question starts to take us down a road away from bond basics and into bond-land proper, with all its different territories and odd products. I don't want to go there, but this is an important (and profitable) distinction, especially for the income investor in a dropping rate environment.

Essentially, a leveraged bond fund borrows money to buy more bonds and uses the new money to increase the yield. For example, say the fund has $100 million in assets and the average yield on that is six percent. Then they borrow $20 million against the $100 million portfolio and use the additional money to get a slightly better yield, say 6.9 percent. If the fund is earning 6.9 percent and borrowing at 4.9 percent, the fund gets that advantage. The risk is that the short end of the yield curve exceeds the long-term.

If short-term interest rates go to eight percent, the fund is losing money. If they go to 1 percent, yield jumps up impressively. This can create some instability of income as short-term interest rates fluctuate and increase the fund's interest payments.

☛ *Leveraged Funds During the Wealth Shift*

Obviously, these funds are highly sensitive to interest rates, and I see those rates dropping heading into the Wealth Shift and staying low. So if the fund has a large inventory of higher-yielding bonds, it can probably leverage them and bump their yields up. That's a good thing, but not a sure thing.

Final Note on Bonds: It's All Relative

In thinking about the rate swings on bonds, remember that a little drop can mean a lot. When interest rates go from six percent to five percent, it's a one-percent swing, but as a percentage, it's twelve percent. If interest rates are at two percent and they drop to one percent, it's still a one-percent drop, but rates are dropping by half. Bond prices will go up substantially more when interest rates go from two percent to one percent than they would go from five percent to six percent. It's the relative change, not the absolute change, that matters. A quarter-point drop in interest rates when they're at 1.5 percent is huge, the same as a full point when rates are at six percent. The bond market will react positively or negatively (and blindingly fast) to even small changes in that environment—an important fact to keep in mind in the low-rate environment of the Wealth Shift.

Mortgages and Mortgage-Backed Securities: Uncertainty in the House

Mortgages are income investments that come with a surprising degree of uncertainty for income investors. It's not that they fail to deliver a good yield; in fact, they usually pay more than a CD or money market. And they can be very safe if federal agencies like the FHA, VA, Fannie Mae, or Freddie Mac are guaranteeing or underwriting the loans. The problem with mortgages is that people keep moving or refinancing.

That nice thirty-year mortgage that is going to deliver seven percent a year for thirty years will probably be paid off in seven years. That's the national average for payoff on a thirty-year mortgage, either through refinancing or the sale of the home, both of which essentially pay the outstanding balance with one big check.

You get your money back; now what? Reinvestment risk is the reality you're facing when you were planning on a thirty-year income stream. The key for income investors is *not* to think long-term on these investments. They are, effectively, short-term and intermediate-term vehicles that may have a role in the income investor's portfolio.

☞ *Mortgage Instruments During the Wealth Shift*

Mortgage securities may be the hedge if interest rates actually rise or stay stable. Why? The echo boomers. They're buying their homes now and throughout the decade, which could drive up demand and create upward pressure on rates. The echo boom doesn't have the demographic muscle of their parents, and they don't have anywhere near the wealth. I don't think this population can create enough demand to hold rates up, but they will do their part, and they offer what every investor should include in their portfolio—a hedge.

REITs: Income and Growth, Maybe

REITs are addressed in the previous chapter dealing with real estate investments. REITs *are* income instruments, however. If you skipped over the last chapter in order to get into the income strategies, make sure you jump back and learn about REITs, and especially how I expect them to perform during the Wealth Shift.

Traditional Equities: The Return of the Dividend Stock

As equity values erode during the economic downturn of the Wealth Shift, there will still be sectors and individual stocks that perform well, and one reason will be their ability to earn and pay dividends.

For the past ten to fifteen years, dividends have been a corporate taboo. CEOs don't like to refer to them; boards of directors don't like to talk about them. And why would they? There's no pressure from boomer investors to pay dividends when that income is taxed at the boomers' high rates. The last thing boomer investors want is a dividend that's going to get taxed at somewhere between thirty and forty percent. They would rather the stock appreciates and sell it later and pay a twenty percent capital gains tax while they're in a kinder tax bracket. (And, as we've defined again and again, what those boomers want, they always get, sooner or later.)

Of course, it hasn't always been this way. Dividends used to be the sweetener on Wall Street. Stocks stayed at high values *because* they paid a handsome dividend and continued to appreciate. Think GM, GE, and the utility stocks of the 70s.

☞ *Dividend Stocks During the Wealth Shift*

During the Wealth Shift, CEOs and shareholders will all want the same things they want today. They want the company to grow its assets, grow its market share, and get more productive. Inevitably their success in these is reflected in stock price, and stock price is the best reflection of company health—as well as a primary factor in the executive team's compensation. During the Wealth Shift, many companies will remain in excellent overall health; some will actually grow much stronger. Discounters will do well. Leisure sectors and hotels could tick upward when the retired boomers start to travel.

Companies in health care have real upsides, specifically the medical device and pharmaceutical sectors. But use caution here; the boomers *will* organize against these high-priced providers and push for more legislative controls. Socialized medicine? Maybe, or some version of price controls that keep earnings in check for these companies and could dramatically affect their standings as darlings of Wall Street.

Regardless, there will be profitable companies during the Wealth Shift, and it will be time to start paying those profits out in real time, with dividend checks to boomer income investors, attracting even more when they do.

An Open Letter to CEOs of Public Companies

You've got a tough job.

You have to keep your company growing amid vicious global competition. You have to keep your company improving in the things it does every day. And you have to make sure. Wall Street is impressed with your efforts—and your earnings—so the stock stays high.

Well guess what—it's about to get tougher.

Because the easy way of growing is no longer so easy. You used to just plow those earnings back into the company, and we applauded with every dollar. And when you needed more cash, you just issued new stock that basically cost you nothing. But what if you can't find buyers for those issuances anymore, and the stock price is already down? You'll have to issue debt, which makes us shareholders nervous. Oh, and we still expect growth. Any ideas?

Here's one: Pay a dividend.

Find a balance between steady growth and consistent dividends. And I'm not talking 1 percent here; I'm talking 4 percent or 5 percent, or more. Something that looks good when compared to bonds. That will bring in the boomer investors who are interested in income, and it will keep the growth investors around who are interested in appreciation.

Like I said, it's not going to be easy, especially in the tough times that will accompany the baby boomers' retirement, but if you can get it done, your board of directors will be happy your employees will be happy, and Wall Street will make you a celebrity.

You'll also see a few more zeroes in that all-important bonus. It's a tough job, all right. But one that pays real dividends.

Good luck. I, along with about 70 million baby boomers, will be watching very closely.

Sincerely,
Chris Brooke

Reading Ahead: A Short Course in Picking Good Dividend Stocks

If you're looking for dividends over growth, picking stocks doesn't get any easier. It's difficult to tell which companies are likely to pay, and how much. It's a decision that takes into account all the business factors analysts look for when predicting growth, but the board of directors makes the call. How can you tell if a company is dividend-friendly?

First, look at the trends. Look at their track record of dividend payment as earnings have increased or decreased. Read the annual report, specifically the CEO's letter. They may state it outright in their annual report: we plan on increasing dividends. And tell your advisor to do his homework. Dividend trends are harder to predict than traditional growth because they depend on both earnings and the mood of the board, but as income investors grow in number, companies will be making their dividend intentions clearer.

Preferred Stocks: Interesting Hybrids

Preferred shares are part stock and part bond. And for income investors before and during the Wealth Shift, they may also be just the right combination of each.

When a company issues preferred stock, it is issuing a form of equity. Usually there are no voting rights, but not always. Like traditional equities, preferred stocks can be sold at any time.

Yet, like bonds, preferred shares pay a fixed dividend (while bond payments are called interest), whereas common shareholders get whatever dividend the board of directors says they're going to get. Preferred shareholders get a fixed-rate dividend. So if preferred shares are issued at 4 percent, you're going to get 4 percent on the par value of those shares.

What makes this investment even more attractive to income investors is that preferred shares generally don't move up or down with the success of the company. Preferred shareholders get 4 percent in good times and bad. So preferred shares respond to the interest rate environment much like bonds, minus the maturity date.

Preferred shares also have a clear appeal to the companies that choose to issue them: they don't show as a liability on the balance sheet since they don't have to be paid back (remember, there's probably no maturity, so no payback day). Sure, they have the obligation of the dividend, but that's shown as an expense, not a liability, and analysts like expenses over debts.

The downside is that most preferred shares, like bonds, have call dates. It's a liability that some companies may be anxious to discharge as they discharge a debt. But in fact, most preferred stocks stay on the market a long, long time, making them an investment worth a close look from income investors in any economic environment, and especially during the Wealth Shift.

Convertible Preferred: The Best of Both

Convertible preferred shares resemble preferred shares, except that you are allowed to convert your shares into the underlying common stock. So the stock trades two ways. It trades on the dividend yield like a bond, and also on the advantage of the underlying common stock's potential. If its number ticks up, you can convert and gain some appreciation.

The price of having the upside option is a lower yield . . . generally money market kinds of yields. But if an income investor wants a way back into a rising stock, a convertible share is the right choice.

Covered Call Writing

There are more than two ways (selling and dividends) to make money off of a stock portfolio, and covered call writing is one. It's a form of options; it's a more active and aggressive tactic, and here's how it works.

Let's say you have 100,000 shares of XYZ that have appreciated greatly since you bought them, but you're not particularly interested in selling. Yet you want some income now, so you sell an option on that stock, or you "write an option."

What this option does is give someone the right to buy that stock from you at a set price during a certain period, usually six months. Let's say your XYZ stock is at $50 a share and you sell the right to buy your stock at $60 a share—that's called the strike price. For that option to buy, you are paid $2 a share, or $200,000.

The upside is the stock doesn't get to $60 and you pocket the $200,000 as a nice piece of income. Then you can reissue the option again and, you hope, keep it going.

The downside is the stock runs up to $72—or even $92—and you're forced to sell your shares at $60. You still made a bunch of money and get to keep the 200K—not a bad downside. Tax implications? You bet. Both on the premium and the stock price gains. But a profit is a profit.

The prices are all set on the options market, and are a reflection of what the market thinks about that stock and the market at the time. The "strike" price is the price when the option kicks in, and the "premium" is the price per share to buy that call option. In a tough market, calls are close to actual market prices and premiums are low. In an appreciating market, everything's more expensive, including options.

Covered call writing works well for investors who have, over a lifetime of investing, accumulated large numbers of shares that have greatly appreciated. They may not be motivated to sell those and buy bonds. Or they may have a bond portfolio for some income, but the majority of their future retirement income is tied up in stocks—stocks that may not be paying dividends. If the option is at a price they would take anyway, and the income is necessary now, call option writing is an effective tactic.

☞ *Covered Call Writing During the Wealth Shift*

During the bear market of the Wealth Shift—when many investors migrate from growth to income, and the equity markets see reduced growth overall—covered call writing may prove especially effective. Income investors will be looking for every opportunity to generate cash flow, and growth investors will be looking for bargains. Could be a great time for income investors with the right kind of portfolios. At the same time, these instruments will be affected by a bear market that will shrink premiums and reduce spreads.

International Debt

In the weakened U.S. economy of the Wealth Shift, when rates remain low on bonds and other debt instruments, income investors may find higher yields overseas. The first places to look will be the Far East and the Near Far East, or China and Japan, and India.

Earlier in the book, we explored the dynamics of Japan's economy and the eventual recovery from its own Wealth Shift. Indeed, the rising sun will be rising again. Along with it, interest rates and the demand for money.

As their recovery finally gets some traction and the dollar remains strong against the yen, that moment will be the right one to buy the highest-yielding Japanese debt. Then as the dollar weakens during the Wealth Shift, the yen strengthens (the two currencies are usually moving in different directions). So not only do investors have a higher-yielding asset in yen-dominated terms, those yen actually convert to a higher number of dollars than when first invested.

It can mean a good, stable income stream through a foreign currency that is getting stronger than ours, but it's not without risk. In fact, it's speculative. But if the Japanese economy recovers as predicted, there *will* be debt opportunities for income investors. Then there's China.

While Japan is one of the most efficient capitalist nations, China is still struggling with the transition from communism to capitalism. This creates both more opportunities and more risk.

There will be more and more debt issuance opportunities coming out of China in the near term, especially as its membership and participation in the Word Trade Organization gathers momentum. And of course, in many parts of China they're already moving pretty fast. Capital is starting to flow more freely there, and money is coming in to fund the infrastructure growth. It's speculative as well, more so than Japanese debt, but it also hold the promise of high yields in a beneficial currency exchange.

In India, a technical service infrastructure is developing that might surprise most American investors. Millions of customer service calls are routed there each day, and the English-speaking group within their massive population is leading a technical revolution that's creating jobs, skilled workers, and investment opportunities. There are debt issues every day by companies building the infrastructure in India. Risks and uncertainties abound, and good advice is essential, but there will be opportunities as the Wealth Shift squeezes U.S. companies and forces even greater efficiencies.

Income investors with an international view may also be thinking about Europe. It's a great place to vacation, but I wouldn't look for good debt opportunities there for some time. The euro is unstable, the European Union is fractured, and their currencies—whatever they are—usually move in the same direction as the dollar. There may be good issuances coming out of England and Germany, and perhaps Ireland and France, but past that, income investors can do better either right here, or in Asian markets.

☛ *International Investing During the Wealth Shift*

Start with the guidelines and concerns detailed above, and get the help of an advisor who knows the territory. You probably wouldn't travel there without the help of a travel agent. Don't send your money there without an experienced guide as well.

CDs and Other Short-Term Instruments: Handy in the Right Hands

For income investors, CDs, money markets, and savings accounts are all classified as short-term investments. They can be helpful, but not particularly attractive given the low interest rates that will accompany the Wealth Shift. Still, there are always going to be wise uses for these instruments, regardless of the interest rate environment.

They're great for predetermined liquidity needs. Buy a CD for eighteen months when you know that eighteen months from now you will have a cash need . . . maybe a big tax bill or a tuition payment. When the money is destined for a certain purchase or expense, then preservation is essential and reinvestment risk is irrelevant. You're not going to be reinvesting the money because, essentially, you've already spent it.

As for money market instruments, they are only effective for short-term liquidity and emergency funds: the three to six months of living expenses all good planners want you to have immediately available. These instruments will always pay modest rates of return relative to the current environment. In any rate environment, you find a better return elsewhere.

Liquidity and Safety . . .

CDs and money market accounts protect your principal with a guarantee from the federal government. If your bank fails and the government can't come up with your money, we're all in bad shape.

Money market and savings accounts are pure liquidity. CDs have always been understood as limiters on liquidity, but that isn't always true. Some CDs are surprisingly liquid. There are marketable CDs that are bought and sold on the open market. Banks won't sell them because they play hell with the balance sheet, but they can be purchased at just about any brokerage house. You'll earn a few basis points less, but you can get your money back without paying the dreaded "penalty for early withdrawal."

Sharp advisors will steer their clients toward a marketable CD with a longer term and, hence, a higher rate even if the money will be needed before the maturation date—get the five-year yield but plan on selling it in three. If rates are the same or lower at three years, the investors sell the CD and pocket almost every dollar they would have made in five years. If rates rise, the option to sell remains, but it may not justify the loss. Either way, it's good to have a choice.

But with Significant Reinvestment Risks

Income investors during any economic period are facing reinvestment risks when they rely on short-term instruments to generate their income. Even in periods of consistently high interest rates, the rates can fluctuate quite a bit during any three-, four-, or five-year period. With every tick downward, essential future income is at risk. If you're going to live twenty years in retirement and you have a large portion of your money locked into in CDs that mature in five years, you're facing huge reinvestment risk.

The Strategies

Planning Concepts for Income Investors Before and During the Wealth Shift

The go-go mentality that drove the market expansion of the late 1990s and early 2000s has given way to a more cautious approach. That's a good thing, even if a lot of people had to get knocked on their butts to get here. But just because investors are looking more closely at bonds and other less-volatile instruments, that doesn't mean we're all ready to be killer income investors. My yet-to-retire clients— many of whom are sharp market watchers—are universally underinformed on the basics of income investing. And many brokers are just plain dumb on the topic.

You have to know the tools, and you need a strategy.

Developing an Income Strategy

Planning is essential to income investing. While growth investment planning (especially for younger investors) can almost be summed up as "earn more now and we'll figure out what to do with it later," income investing that isn't carefully planned and managed is going to fail. And failure at this period of your life has immediate and extremely serious consequences.

In this section, we'll explore specific income investing strategies for both before and during the Wealth Shift. They can be put in practice if you're retired now and investing for income, and if your retirement is nearing and you are beginning to transition from growth to income. Each requires the guidance of a knowledgeable financial advisor, especially as the Wealth Shift approaches and the game gets a lot harder.

Buy and Hold

This strategy delivers long-term, fixed income. Bonds with long maturities are usually the foundation of this portfolio, and they are held until maturity or until circumstances necessitate a sale. While their value may appreciate or depreciate based on rate fluctuations, they are held through it all, continually delivering that interest payment as living income.

The advantage is peace of mind that comes from a consistent, long-term income. But these instruments will eventually mature, bringing reinvestment risks with them. The income can also be eroded by inflation. With no new income to offset the rising costs of goods, quality of life can suffer. And what if rates climb past what you're earning and stay there for a while? Could be tough to watch.

During the Wealth Shift, this simple strategy could look pretty smart if you've gotten into long bonds early or at the top of a rate wave. Inflation probably won't be a factor, so your buying power will stay constant. It's not my favorite strategy, but it works great for some clients who are extremely risk-averse and hands-off. If that's you, talk to your advisor about the right time to start stocking your bond portfolio.

Reallocation and Opportunistic Sale

The foundation here is a well-diversified portfolio and the careful attention of you and your advisor. Regardless of the specific allocation, this strategy calls for periodic rebalancing. For example, a person might have 65 percent bonds, thirty percent stocks, and five percent cash. Then, take a periodic look—every six months to a year—at the performance of each individual instrument. In a balanced portfolio, there is usually a winner somewhere. Capture those profits, take out the income needed and reallocate to your weaker positions.

During the Wealth Shift, this strategy could have people biting their nails. The boomers' retirement could easily hold the equity market's growth down, or stop it altogether. Which means your allocation model should have limited equity exposure from 2007 through the next decade.

Income and Sell

This is a common strategy for income investors in my practice. It's based on the answers to two simple questions: What do you need? and, What do you want?

To answer the first question, we determine their basic needs right down to the dollar. If they need $5,000 a month to pay bills, debts, greens fees . . . you know, the essentials . . . then we put together a portfolio of long-term fixed instruments that generate $60,000 a year with no volatility of income, and we never touch it. That portfolio will have some combination of intermediate and long-term treasuries; we might use long-term municipals; and we might use high-grade long-term corporate bonds with very few call features. Then we get to work on the second question: What do you want?

Say that another $60,000 is desired for travel, luxury purchases, and gifts. If this money appears, it's spent on these things. If not, oh well . . . there's always next year. This portfolio might include instruments that create cash flow, like REITs and even carefully selected equities with immediate appreciation potential. If they do appreciate, they are sold, and the profits are turned into an African safari or an Alaskan cruise, or both.

Income and liquidity. Needs and wants. A very solid strategy that I've put in place for many of my clients.

During the Wealth Shift, I see this strategy continuing its viability. If the bond portfolio was built right, income stays consistent and beats the yields of the market. Inflation should stay in the background and things should be okay for this investor. Can they be better than okay? That depends on the markets and the particular performance of the more volatile side of this strategy. The safari may have to wait, but at least there will be roast beef on the table.

Ladder Rotation

Imagine a ladder that extends one rung, stops, then the top rung is removed and attached to the bottom rung. Then again, and again, and so forth. That's a ladder rotation strategy.

It's made up of bonds, CDs, and other fixed maturity investments purchased to create a succession of maturities, year after year. Creating a ten-year ladder is common. Then as the top group matures this year, the principal is used to purchase instruments that mature ten years from now. The interest from all the instruments is taken out through the year as income, but the total principal remains the same.

It's a smart way to protect the majority of your principal from reinvestment risk, and it allows you to relax a bit around the inevitable interest rate fluctuations. The downside, of course, is your lack of liquidity should rising rates pass your current yields.

During the Wealth Shift, falling rates or rates that fall and can't get up are going to reduce the yield that the entire portfolio earns as higher-yielding instruments mature and then drop (quite literally) to the bottom of the rate pile. If rates stay low for a decade, the steady erosion of income could be very problematic.

Fixed Ladder

This laddered strategy also uses fixed-maturity instruments but does not reinvest the principal at the top of the cycle. The Fixed Ladder strategy uses the principal returned at maturity as income. When the checks arrive, they're simply put to work in short-term accounts like money markets while you live the retirement you can afford. Yet, clearly, it can't go on for the course of a lengthy retirement unless the principal is in the many millions.

Instead, this strategy is ideally suited to serve as a bridge from a working income to a pension or a larger retirement disbursement—like from age sixty to official retirement at sixty-five. And it can be done with a relatively modest amount of money. If your bridge was five years, and you could live on $60,000 a year, you could get there with less than $300,000, depending on how much additional interest you were earning and using as income in addition to the principal each year.

It's great when used as directed—easy, safe, and completely immune from reinvestment risk, yet as vulnerable as the next guy to interest-rate drops that reduce interest income, and just as locked in if they climb.

Once the Wealth Shift hits, you're in about the same position as before: consistent, short-term income, and some vulnerability to rate volatility but probably not enough to abandon the strategy altogether. After all, you do have more principal waiting for you at the end of the ladder, right?

Managed Income and Maturities

As we discussed earlier, bonds with long maturities are more valuable as rates are falling. When rates are ticking up, shorter maturities have the most appeal on the market. With this strategy, the sale and purchase of bonds in the portfolio is timed to take advantage of the market demands. And yes, it's not for beginners.

A sharp bond trader can make this strategy hum, earning money on appreciating bonds and keeping effective yields competitive with anything on the market. But even the Masters of the Universe aren't going to be able to keep income consistent from year to year, or even month to month.

During the Wealth Shift, the same goes double. You need a crack advisor and a lot of flexibility. In the end, for many income investors, this strategy could be the path to some very impressive returns.

Chapter 5
Investing for Growth: A New Emphasis on Value and Income

Successful growth investing during the Wealth Shift will necessitate that investors change their focus. First and foremost, they'll need to buy and then sell the instruments that aging and retired boomers will be searching for, if not fighting for—income investments, in other words. That's where the chapter begins.

Growth investors will need to move value and earnings to the very first question they ask about a investment—those are questions growth investors have often neglected in the recent past—and evaluate the potential for future earnings in the context of this very different demographic environment: Club Meds will falter. Golf resorts will explode.

And growth investors will need to greatly expand their worldview. The same demographic movements that will dominate the economy and bedevil the legislators will coincide with the continued strengthening of several international markets and the emergence of others. You'll still have growth opportunities. They just won't all be growing on the trees in your own backyard. Later in the chapter, we'll take a tour.

There are a handful of aggressive strategies that I'll introduce here for the growth investor. Short selling, bear funds, and other hedge instruments are going to be in many growth investor's playbooks. I'm not a big fan of these strategies for reasons I'll detail later, but for some late-stage boomers, and even more younger investors they might have a place.

First, Growth Defined

Growth investing, simply investing, is something that you believe will appreciate over time. It's a simple idea, of course, but it's the "over time" part that complicates the issue as much as the uncertainty of appreciation.

It's tempting, comforting even, to think of growth in linear and predictable terms, just like time itself. Bad idea. Markets in all their forms simply do not perform in a linear model. Even real estate markets, which are among the more reliably predictable markets, are prone to very nonlinear fluctuations. During the Wealth Shift, market fluctuations, or the lack thereof, will challenge investors and their advisors to maintain growth.

Equities markets in particular laugh at your sensible, linear predictions. They are usually either doing extremely well or extremely poorly. They almost never perform at the average, which is an awareness you need to bring to any investment strategy that optimistically aims for growth consistent with market averages. The former U.S. Secretary of Labor, Robert Reich, who stands a diminutive 4' 10" often warns people to be wary of averages by quipping that he and 7' 1" Shaquille O'Neal have an average height of nearly 6 feet. He wishes it were true, no doubt, but averages do not replace the original data points.

The same is true in the U.S. equities markets. An analysis of the market's performance over an eighty-year period reveals that the market only moves in the mean less than 5 percent of the time. So if the market has averaged 11 percent growth over eighty years, the returns in any given year between 9 percent and 13 percent have been realized in about four years out of eighty.

Markets move to sharp extremes or not at all. They are in the high double digits or the negative, or they are flat. Very flat. In 1928, the Dow hit 300. After the 1929 crash, the market fell drastically to, at one point, below 100. It was not until 1954 that the Dow ended the year above 300 again. That's thirty-two years of minimal market growth following a period of wild speculation. Modern-day speculators in 1999 and early 2000 might have looked ahead (grinning ear to ear) to a 15,000 Dow. We may yet hit that, but in twenty years we could easily be seeing a Dow just about where it is today.

The Boom before the Shift

For the middle years in this decade, boomers will be bringing their dollars out of safer, fixed return assets for one more run at traditional growth. That move aiming to make up for lost ground creates an upside for everyone in equities, including the late-stage boomers who are ten, fifteen years, or more away from retirement.

Once confidence rises to a certain tipping point, several trillion dollars that is now cooling it in money markets earning half a percent is going to flood in. What's more, the boomers are poised to collect a few trillion more in their inheritances that is also—given the depression-shaped tendencies of their parents—playing it safe in banks and bonds. There's one more boom market for the boomers to ride, and growth investors everywhere ought to be along for the ride, short as it may be.

Domestic Strategies for Growth Investors

See the Bear, Don't Fear It

In 1965, the Dow was 969, and it didn't hit that high mark again until eight years later, in 1972. In 2003, as I write this, NASDAQ stands about where it was in 1996. Seven years of zero net growth. Long-term bear markets can and will happen, and I'm not being bearish on markets. I'm being a realist, like all investors should be as we head into the Wealth Shift. And that also means holding the demographic facts close at hand, beginning with the historical.

As mentioned in an earlier chapter, the dizzying returns of the late 1990s were exceeded only by those of the 1920s. During that decade, the market grew over 300 percent. Then, immediately following this massive market surge, the entire economy collapsed—not just the market valuations, the entire economy. Speculation and a cockeyed banking system didn't cause all the carnage. Millions of immigrant consumers left the economy by retiring or dying, and the people left to buy the goods weren't there in sufficient numbers to support the production. A population shift was at the root of the Great Depression. It will be at the root of the Wealth Shift.

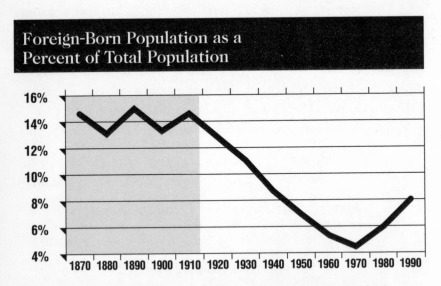

Foreign-Born Population as a Percent of Total Population

The shaded area indicates how numerous foreign born individuals were in the pre-Depression economy. They were consumers and producers of essential goods. When a large percentage of them retired—or died, or both—in the early 1920s, the stage was set for the great depression. Our own boomers will have a similar impact.

U.S. Census Bureau Population Division

Don't fear bear markets—it's unproductive and distracting. Instead, embrace them as naturally occurring events that can also create huge opportunities. Sure, the stock that was trading a few years ago at four times the current price, or higher, may still be a good investment for growth-oriented players. "Buy low and sell high" wasn't just meant to comically oversimplify the difficult work of equity investing, but the buying low *can be* easy in bear markets. And selling high can be pretty easy too, if you've bought both low and smart.

I can hear your next question from here: What to buy? Let's move on, beginning with a quick look back.

Today's Value Is Tomorrow's Growth

Value has come back into vogue recently as investors have returned to more rational investment disciplines. What we might still currently call a growth stock is putting whatever earnings they can generate back into the company's growth. Value stocks are about company growth, but they are also broadly financed, and established enough to pay a dividend without derailing their forward progress.

In the Wealth Shift, what we now call large cap value will actually provide the growth that attracts growth investors. The well-allocated portfolio heading into the Wealth Shift should have a component of assets dedicated to U.S. domestic equities: large cap, small cap, value, and growth.

As the Wealth Shift progresses, growth investors should migrate to more large cap value, with dividends. That's where the domestic appreciation will come from.

Get Growth by Buying Income

In the previous chapter, we took you into income investing with the assumption that you, like most baby boomers and everyone younger, have had little experience with these strategies and vehicles. We've all been all about the growth, and you may still be. But you'll soon be in the minority.

During the Wealth Shift income investments will be essential to millions of baby boomers, so if you skipped over that chapter as you charged ahead into this one, consider a quick reversal of course. The more you know about income investing, the better growth investor you'll be during the coming shift.

As trillions of dollars begin their inevitable shift into income instruments, those instruments will become more valuable. Simple supply and demand. You want to be holding the finite supply and selling to the growing demand. In this case, the supply is income-earning investments, be they dividend-paying equities, certain bonds, and perhaps some equities in sectors that will be performing well enough to attract cautious income investors—more on those later. But my larger point is this: Growth investors during the Wealth Shift will succeed by selling income instruments that they bought ahead of the boomer demand.

Undeniable Fact #1:
Boomers Will Need Income from Investments

Retired life is off the clock. No boss and no paycheck. But it's not free. People who retire still need income. In the Wealth Shift, many of those traditional income sources for retirees will be weakened, faltering, or evaporated. Traditional pension funds are already in trouble. Social Security is a big question, and even a full payout from the SSA won't go far for those go-go boomers in retirement. What's more, interest rates will be at, or near, historic lows, so the stable CDs and other fixed-return instruments will be paying anemic returns.

Just like the boomers created the demand for baby food when they were babies, and minivans when they had their own, they're going to create a demand for high-income-producing assets beginning even now, and accelerating quickly throughout the decade. That is not a question; it is not a maybe. It is a fact.

Undeniable Fact # 2:
Boomer Demand Will Strengthen Certain Sectors

It's a central point in this book, and one worth making again here. Baby boomers in retirement will create enormous revenue opportunities for companies and for entire sectors that are focused on serving their needs.

For growth investors, it will require a very different bias—the consumer sectors will be understood as poles. On one end is the echo boomers, and their location in the Consumer Spending Progression. On the other end is the baby boomers, who are more numerous, wealthier, and more predictable. As boomers move out of one macro consumptive phase (their work life), they will become more conservative in both their personal spending and their investing. The tricked-out PDA and the technology company that makes it will have little appeal to boomer shoppers and investors.

Put the two undeniable facts together—income-generating securities and boomer-oriented sectors—and let's move ahead.

Undeniable Fact #3:
Bonds Are OK Equity Dividends Will Be Better

Now it gets more difficult. Because interest rates are going to be in the low single digits, the effective yield on bonds are going to stay close to the ground, too. Remember one of the bond basics discussed in the previous chapter. The bond market is ruthlessly efficient at pricing bonds so their effective yields are kept at or near current rates.

Income is income, and boomers will want bonds. But growth investors who buy bonds now, or soon, probably won't realize the kinds of gains that they would if they're selling dividend-paying equities, or equities that *will* be paying one in the future. Got your crystal ball out? You won't need it. Just think demographics and watch the dividend practices unfolding now.

Start with the companies paying a dividend now. Their numbers are already increasing. In January of 2003, the ultimate technology start-up, Microsoft, announced that it would join the ranks of stocks appealing to "widows and retirees" and begin paying a dividend.

The Microsoft dividend of 16 cents per share won't launch many yachts, but it does signal a new emphasis on turning revenue and earnings into direct and immediate returns for shareholders. Microsoft isn't the first in this new wave, and they won't be the last.

Growth investors will do well to identify and investigate the companies that are paying a dividend now and will be able to increase that dividend over time, as well as the companies and sectors that will be paying dividends in the future. If you recall from the Income Investing chapter, dividends are likely to become the price that CEOs and boards of directors are willing to pay to keep their stock price high. They're reading the demographic charts, just like you are, and they understand the changing nature of boomer investors.

In mid-2003, Congress passed a bill that cut taxes on dividends, among other things. The Bush administration wanted more, but the outcome reflects a growing appreciation of just how much boomer voters matter as they approach their own dividend-earning days. Boomers will continue to drive the issue once they realize how important dividends can be to their income portfolios.

Here's the bottom line: Boomers will need income in retirement. Many companies and sectors will perform well in their service to boomer buyers. Those are the companies and sectors that will be able to pay healthy dividends. Buy them before the boomers realize they need them, and sell them at a profit. I call that growth.

The Three Doors

Growth may be waiting behind three different doors. The first looks like the front door to your house, the second is a grand amphitheater entrance, and the third is a glass door, with a helpful receptionist at the desk. Let's open each.

Self-Managed: Your Decisions. Your Biases. You're on Your Own.

You can make your own investment decisions without ever talking to a broker or advisor. Especially today, with the financial information infrastructure still in place from the 90s boom and the explosion of day trading. You have the data and access to pages of opinion and analysis. The CNBC feed can be a window on your computer desktop. You also have your own biases that are shaping every decision you make, sometime subtly, often overtly.

Those same biases that have helped you pick good companies (which, thankfully, is not really that difficult) also prevents you from selling them when you should. Maybe you don't want to pay taxes on the gains or you're sure it will bounce back. Fine, but what's the investment discipline at work here? Often, there's very little. Which can dramatically soften the growth curve of an entire portfolio, even one that is well-balanced.

It's possible to be a lone wolf here and still get some help from a pro—a broker or other adviser—but even that advice is shaped by the biased questions you ask, how fully informed the advisor is of your goals and situation, and by how faithfully you follow their suggestions.

If you like the game, and have some mad money, go have fun. But bring your big money down the street to one of the remaining doors.

Publicly Managed: You and Everybody Else

This is growth for the masses, literally . . . a huge amphitheater with the gates wide open and someone waving you in. These are mutual funds, mostly, chosen from the giant menu board of funds available to all investors. These funds are headed by a manager, who is a manager in name only. A more accurate title might be "Group Appeaser." These public fund managers (I call them "public" not because they are connected to a government, but because the funds themselves are open to the general public, anyone with the minimum investment) are beholden to the group, not to any one investor. When their equity holdings dip, they sell at the very moment they probably should be buying. That's because their investors are leaving and need to be paid. When their holdings tick up, instead of selling to capture some yield, they have to buy because investors are bringing them cash. It's all about cash flow.

Obviously these funds are fine choices for millions of investors, and their managers are sharp pros. It's just that if you had the option, you'd probably rather hire them to focus their expertise on you individually. Which gets us to the next door.

The Privately Managed Portfolio: Tapping the Best Minds

In a privately managed portfolio, you hold the securities and you get the benefit of professional fund managers. It's what investors of substantial worth are now doing. They, or their main advisor, hire a manager to manage a single aspect of their portfolio. They hand the large cap value allocations to a manager with an appealing approach to large cap value. Same with small cap growth, bonds, and international.

These managers make good decisions at the right time for each client. You want to capture some gains? Pick up the phone and talk about it, one-on-one. Over coffee, in a paneled office.

It's what pension funds have been doing for decades. Now, with the boomer's remarkable accumulation of wealth, with more to come, individual investors are realizing the advantages of this investment model.

And no matter which door you enter, always have an independent advisor nearby. They add value by balancing your biases with a true investment discipline. If you've got it bad for pork bellies, they won't top you from throwing your money in the pork belly market. A good advisor will, however, present the facts on how pork bellies compare with other investments, and offer alternatives to pork bellies that might just satisfy your hunger for gains without exposing you to that potential mess.

Sector Watch: Looking Ahead, Buying Now

Before working our way into specific sectors and industries, I want to reinforce one of the essential differences between growth investing of the past and growth investing in the context of the Wealth Shift.

Investors going for growth in the 1990s were looking at equities in a completely different light than boomer investors of the mid-2000s and beyond. Then, buyers were moving stocks on an untested hybrid of sector strength, unseen potential, and buzz. Revenue and earnings took a backseat and dividends weren't even in the car. Blame whom you want, but everyone shares some of it: buyers, sellers, bankers, brokers, board, whiz-kid CEOs, and the option-grabbing employees who helped make the Dow and NASDAQ America's #1 spectator sport.

I heard a money manager once say it is no longer about price to earnings; it is about price to concept—an idea as reckless as it is silly. Fundamentals have always mattered. Earnings and profit have always mattered, and in the Wealth Shift, they will be looked at under a harsh, realistic light by both income and growth investors, and by the advisors they engage to help them. As for Mr. "Price to Concept," let's hope he's either seen the light or was shown the door.

Back to earnings: Why do they matter more now? It's simple: Companies without strong earnings won't be able to pay attractive dividends. That spectacular 22 percent rise in earnings better be accompanied by a similar rise in the dividend, or income-hungry boomers investors won't be all that interested. Good companies performing at exceptional levels—but resistant to paying dividends—could actually get left behind in a market rise that favors companies that share their profits in quarterly checks to shareholders.

Sector to Watch: Health Care for Aging Boomers

At my seminars, I often ask the group what companies are going to perform well as the boomers cross into retirement. It's a softball question, and they always make contact: "health care," "insurance," "pharmaceuticals," "medical devices," "hospitals." Someone once said "plastic surgery" and they could be right . . . never underestimate the willingness of this group to pay someone to help them stay young. No one, as you might guess, says "wireless modems" or "designer fashions."

It makes sense, obviously, with millions of boomers heading into their sixties, there will be an increase in the base demand for health care. Revenues will follow, and the smart CEOs and boards of directors will authorize dividend payments to go along with their new spending in R & D.

But before you buy, consider a few additional factors. These companies and sectors also pose a clear risk in the form of legislative and insurance muddling. The government doesn't want to pay retail for Medicare, and Medicare is already beginning to dominate the discussion when the planners and budget teams sit down to talk at hospitals and pharmaceutical companies. Just wait until millions of boomers begin entering the Medicare program. The government response to health care companies could well limit their growth, their revenues, and their dividends—all bad things for investors in these sectors.

Some providers (hospitals, physician groups, surgery centers, etc.) are aiming to sidestep the entire issue by dealing with private pay patients exclusively. That avoids one problem while creating another: better care and access for those with resources. Poor care and very limited access for the many millions who have much fewer resources. "But that's already happening now," you say? Keep watching. It could get very ugly.

Private pay insurance companies will also have a say in how health care gets paid. The relationship between insurers and providers is more collaborative in nature, but it could still result in reduced revenues for the companies investors are looking to for growth.

☞ *Health Care Equities During the Wealth Shift*

The huge demand can't be ignored as a positive factor in looking at these securities. But a lot of companies are entering this space hoping to serve the needs of aging boomers, which challenges each to stay competitive and viable. Look for new services, products, and ideas developed to meet the many needs. Innovation still rules here, even if the patients are not innovators themselves. Risks: Government changes in how Medicare pays could reduce earnings and dampen innovation. Millions of new Medicare patients could destabilize an already offbalance situation. When following these stocks, don't skip over the front page on your way to the business section. Politics and population will be stirring the health care sector as much as science. And if a company can't deliver the earnings that can be distributed as a dividend (or just won't commit to one), keep shopping. Growth investors are looking for other people's future income needs as the source for that growth. No income, no grow.

Sector to Watch: Leisure and Entertainment

With over 70 million of them, you can expect a staggering variety of retirement lifestyles. Many will be able to vacation on the Mediterranean. Many, many more will be just spending a few days at the boater's lake one state over. Either way, business will be responding to an increased demand for leisure and entertainment. There will be infrastructure needs, product needs, content needs, and communication needs. It's going to get busy for the companies who can help the boomers relax.

A handful of REITs that specialize in golf have been formed already. Their collective market performance has been in the rough so far, but golf is riding a wave of popularity and the entire golf industry is looking ahead with an unmistakable bounce in its step. Golf REITs and other specialized trusts will begin to debut. Keep watching the real estate media and be ready. It may be a while before those REITs are paying a dividend, but I see the sector with a lot of muscle to create revenue. In the probable bear market of the Wealth Shift, consistent and growing revenue will be rewarded with rises in the stock price.

Casinos and gaming companies are winning with customers and investors. Profits have been climbing in the casinos and hotels, and even companies that make the slot machines have been showing consistent growth with the addition of new casinos and gambling riverboats. There's a lot of competition for the gambling dollar these days, which is just setting the table for millions of boomers looking for something to do with their pocket change, be it $200 or $20,000. Watch these stocks now, and be ready to get in the game. These companies are mature enterprises, so a dividend is not a long shot.

Who's hurting? The movie and music business has suffered with the aging of their core customers for the past forty years. Traffic and dollars spent at amusement parks has been down, too. The uneasiness of the past few years is often cited for a reason. And while that's true to some degree, what's missed in the analysis is the demographic reality: The vast majority of the boomer's kids are past the age of teacup rides and even roller coasters. Once again, the boomers drove supply past the point of demand, and now everyone is wondering what happened. The answer is, quite simply, life.

☞ *Entertainment and Leisure Equities During the Wealth Shift*

Watch for specialized REITs in everything from golf to marinas to RV parks. And if a company is in the business of making toys that retirees will want in their garages, homes, or hands, start your research now and be ready to move quickly once the Wealth Shift gains momentum. One thing that you already know is that gambling will always win as a leisure activity for millions of people, and millions more are waiting for their chances. During the Wealth Shift, companies in this sector will have a lot of potential for growth, given the demographics alone. Stay clear of leisure and entertainment aimed at a younger demographic. There *are* millions of echo boomers, I but there is also a ruthless competition for their entertainment dollars that is holding down growth in the entire industry.

Also, be mindful of the larger risks associated with all consumer-oriented equities during the Wealth Shift—a soft economy will diminish the discretionary income for millions of people, boomers and everyone else.

Sector to Watch: Construction and Infrastructure

Residential and commercial construction companies aren't all small outfits made up of guys who have grown up on the jobsite. Many are large and profitable enterprises with long track records as public companies. There are companies that specialize in homes, hospitals, retirement communities, golf and tennis clubs—you get the idea. These are the construction stocks to research and watch, especially the ones with good penetration in the South and Southwest.

The low interest rate environment of the Wealth Shift will help these companies do more for less, just as it will help their boomer buyers. They are extremely efficient businesses to begin with. It takes a lot of equipment to build a building, but these companies own very little of it. A well-managed construction company has surprisingly small capital expenses, so profits can go quickly to the bottom line, and the best of them are, or will be, in a position to pay that dividend, which will obviously elevate their stocks significantly.

☞ *Construction Equities During the Wealth Shift*

Find the companies now who are well-positioned (both geographically and with the business model) to respond to boomer demand. Dividends will strengthen the argument for bringing some of these securities into your growth portfolio.

Back to Bonds, Briefly

The basic counsel I offer of buying what the boomers are going to want holds true with bonds. If you see a long-term bond that's paying six percent, or a ten-year CD at 5.5 percent, particularly a marketable CD, buy it. Treasuries are popular in these uncertain times, which has eroded some of the effective yields. Yet, these are the income instruments the boomers will be wanting in their portfolios, in part because of their stability.

Corporates and even junk are finding buyers aplenty now, and will continue to. Rates like 9 percent and more have a way of attracting a crowd in low-rate, bear markets. Use caution here, however. The ability of these companies to stay strong and current on their debt payments is not at all certain, especially during the soft economy of the Wealth Shift.

As a growth investor aiming to sell to boomers, the instruments are only as good as their income provided. (Forgive my continual hammering of this point; however, if you remember only one growth strategy for the years ahead, this should be it.)

☞ Bonds During the Wealth Shift

As the previous chapter illustrates, there will be good opportunities in corporate and junk. Many companies will succeed wildly and will be issuing debt to fund their growth, not stock. Use discipline here, and measure every high-rate corporate by its ability to keep paying that rate in the new environment of the Wealth Shift. As for U.S. treasuries and municipals, the income checks will keep going out, which boomers will depend on, but the bond market gods will effectively keep these prices in line.

Repeat after Me: "I'm Not in It for the Income"

For many growth investors, the inclusion of so many income-producing assets is going to be a tempting situation—especially if those equities are rising in market price. The temptation will be to hold and let that money fund something fun. Bad idea. Or maybe just bad timing.

Timing, in fact, will be an essential discipline for growth investors.

Once the dividends fall below other dividend investments, sell it. Your mission is not to hold and collect an income stream. Your mission is to buy, wait for boomers to see the income stream and want to buy it, bid the price up, and once the effective yield drops: sell it. Then find the next investment that those boomers that haven't found and buy it. It's always tempting to maximize returns by waiting one more month, week, or day. Be careful.

You may not have a slow decline to ponder your sale. Long-term bear markets are notable for their significant and rapid drops. A stock that gets overpriced, bringing the effective dividend to almost nothing, can get clobbered in a hurry in a general market decline, which pretty much describes the environment of the Wealth Shift.

International Strategies for Growth Investors

Domestic, income-producing investments won't be the only option for growth investors any more than boomers will be the only buyers you have to appeal to. There will be instruments, sectors, and markets that fit the classic growth model. It's just that many of them will be doing their growing outside the United States.

Retired or soon-to-retire boomers won't be invested internationally to any large degree because these securities are much less likely to generate the income they need. Plus, they make older investors uneasy. Late-stage boomers will include them in their portfolios, but even then, this demographic will probably be the first to maximize their gains or minimize their losses. International investing requires a longer time cycle.

There will be fantastic opportunities to create value, and for the long-term growth investor, regardless of whether they hold a lot of income instruments in their portfolio. For these younger investors, the best (and only) growth game in town may be out of town. Far out.

Out with the Despots, in with the Starbucks

In a book written just after the ball of the Berlin Wall, the author David Halberstam wrote that "The Cold war is over and Japan won." At the time, it looked true. Japanese marketing savvy, technical acumen, and quality processes were the envy of the capitalist nations. An entire industry was born around helping United States and European companies "be more Japanese."

Then the cracks in the Japanese model became apparent, including the one that they simply could not fix: their own Wealth Shift—an aging population that stopped spending, borrowing, and working. While Japan is poised for a youth-driven recovery, the rest of the world is already moving toward something that looks more democratic and less despotic.

Cuba, a "tropical Mayberry" to some, given its lack of contemporary American icons and warm, welcoming population, will soon blossom as a market for American companies and American investors. Castro's long harangue is about over.

And in Iraq, the messy business of helping to bring about a form of self-rule continues with an uncertain final goal, except that the resources of this wealthy nation are now available to enrich the citizens of Iraq, and the companies with the skills to grow there.

My point is this: Despite the global unrest that is dominating the front-page headlines, there is and will continue to be impressive advances in free market growth. Microsoft or GM didn't invent capitalism. The urge to create and expand markets is an inborn human trait that can't be squashed by a regime or transformed by an ideology.

As democracy grows, so grows stability. (If you doubt it is growing, consider that in 1912, there were just a half-dozen or so democracies among the world's nations.) Democracies are slow to go to war. No two nations have ever been to war if they also had a McDonald's on their soil. Trade wars, in the form of protectionism, boycotts, dumping and other commercial/governmental meddling will continue. The "free" in free market may at times seem like an oversimplification, if not an overpromise. Still, growth investors should be vigilant for the international opportunities that will follow the U.S. Wealth Shift.

The New West: The Far East

Do you travel east to get to Japan, Korea, China or anywhere else in Eastern Asia? Not usually. The trip takes you West, over the mythic American Western landscape of promise and new beginnings. You go west to get Far East. I like that metaphor. Just as going west means something important in American history, I think going further west to a new kind of western-style opportunity will mark America's future, before, during, and after the Wealth Shift.

Growth Watch: China

America's status as the world's lone superpower is being challenged by China, and, for the most part, American investors should be cheering them along.

China is a communist nation that is nurturing a capitalist soul. Politically, it's becoming more moderate and more transparent. OK, it's still an oddball, but it's getting easier to deal with, both politically and commercially. Opportunities for growth investors are emerging now, and will explode in the near- to medium-term.

Mao and most of his cronies are gone. Many of the Chinese

ministers were educated somewhere else, and they have brought the principles of democracy and capitalism back home. Their version of democracy and capitalism will be meticulously implemented in their own way, which is to say slowly and patiently. Red tape has become a new kind of iron curtain. Yet, that suits the nation's personality; unlike an American, the average Chinese takes a longer view of things, and accepts change at a slower pace. That pace is about to pick up.

Some estimates say that less than ten percent of Chinese consume Western goods. Those same estimates say than in ten years it will be thirty percent. That's an unprecedented new market, and a huge opportunity for U.S. growth investors and companies to provide products to millions and millions of demanding Chinese consumers.

We think China will be a great opportunity for investments in Chinese companies—in Chinese debt—and in multinational companies based in the U.S. and elsewhere that are prudently increasing their exposure in China.

That last group is essential to the international growth equation, and not just in China. Moreover, you can also factor in mutual funds that buy equities of companies with deep penetration into international markets—they spread the risk, and the reward.

Bottom line: some of the sharpest international growth investing will be in American companies selling their goods and services to international buyers.

The Chinese Stock Market? Could Happen

When China reclaimed Hong Kong, the pessimists saw Chinese tanks rolling through downtown. Didn't happen. The Chinese authorities wrapped some of that famous red tape around some trade practices, but for the most part let Hong Kong be Hong Kong. In fact, they appear to be looking to replicate some version of Hong Kong in every other major city along the coast.

The Chinese are as intelligent as they are industrious. They are involved in one of the most interesting economic experiments that we've ever seen. There will be opportunities in private investments, opportunities to invest in the domestic companies that sell into the Chinese markets, and yes, maybe the beginning of the next decade, you may actually see a Shanghai exchange.

Growth Watch: Japan

The demographic shift that caused much of the economic woe to the late, 80s and 90s, and even into today, is starting to reverse. A more productive work force and more dynamic market is beginning to assert itself. The Japanese echo boom is finally being heard.

Yen-denominated securities have some appeal to growth investors, as do Japanese equities. Japan is a stable nation; it doesn't come with the geo-political risks that a China or Korea or Taiwan comes with. It's speculative, and the long bear market has kept a lot of money out. That's lessening every day. Growth investors should start watching Japan now, and researching the landscape for when the U.S. markets begin to soften.

Growth Watch: Other Nations

India is already a huge labor market for U.S. companies, and as India continues to stabilize politically, growth investors are going to see both private opportunities and public equities there.

Mexican, Central American, and South American markets are a natural progression for the U.S. Turmoil still exists—many South American nations still have a degree of militarism in them, which continues to dissipate. These nations are poised to become important trade partners. Many will have tremendous natural resources, and they have huge potential markets. The Brazilian leisure market is one of the most expansive leisure markets in the world. And remember, those boomers will be ready to travel.

The Dollar's Fall from Grace

The U.S. dollar will be the denominating currency of the world for many years to come. Ask a European the value of a euro or a pound, and they'll measure it in dollars. The dollar is the benchmark and will be until the adoption of a global currency, say 100 years from now, give or take a decade or two. The euro represents the future in currency: easy to manage from a retail and exchange perspective, and strong enough to attract trade to the participating nations.

Vast volumes in global trade and currency transfers are heralding the end of nationalism faster than any political force. Nonisolationist policies are the rule, and the ones that aren't are getting left behind in a hurry.

Risks and Opportunities in Dollars

Currencies will always fluctuate, and that presents a constant risk for investors with money in international transactions and markets. Right now, in mid-2003, the euro is stronger than the dollar, and that may remain so for a while.

In the Wealth Shift environment, I believe the U.S. currency is going to be weak, and that's what is going to create additional opportunities in equities and other investments. As the dollar contracts, other currencies will emerge as a stronger currency. The Yen will strengthen. Many of the Asian currencies may start to take their place alongside the more stable currencies in the world. The ruble, which was a joke a few years ago, is starting to get some more serious consideration as a first-world currency.

☞ *International Strategies During the Wealth Shift*

I'm not going to belabor the points and counsel presented above, much of which was crafted with Wealth Shift strategies in mind. Bottom line: Global trade will be the dominant geopolitical force in this decade and the next. Be mindful of terrorism and other disruptive distractions as they create the fear that can irrationally move *all* markets, ours and theirs. Look to the new West, a.k.a. the Far East (especially China and Japan), for an explosion for growth. There will be opportunities that begin and end over there. There will be companies here that prosper over there. There will be mutual funds that offer various combinations of both. Get smart about these opportunities and be ready to get in.

Aggressive Strategies for Growth Investors

The Wealth Shift will have investors and their advisors scrambling for growth. Not everyone will be holding those high-value, income-producing securities. Not everyone will be comfortable sending their money into international markets. And the younger the investor, the more likely he or she will be up for some of the aggressive strategies that follow.

Short Selling

For growth investors who are investing domestically, selling short may be one of the few ways to realize asset growth during the Wealth Shift.

Quick short-sell reminder for anyone who needs it: Investors who sell a stock short are actually borrowing the stock, usually from a brokerage house. The borrowed stock is then sold at today's price. Now there is a loan, and it's not in dollars, it's in shares. The loan is due within a set time period—sometimes a year, often quicker. If the stock was sold at $50 and it drops to $30, a short seller gleefully puts in a buy order and returns the same amount of shares to the broker's shelf, making a tidy $20 per share because of the drop in price.

I'm not a proponent of short selling; it brings out the worst in certain investors with huge short positions that are not yet profitable. Rumors can spread quickly online and can be used as weapons to sink a stock without real justification.

I also don't like how short selling takes away the option to hold a stock. Investors holding a short position are forced to sell on a short timeline, no matter what the stock is doing or not doing. They better have guessed right, because the punishment for guessing wrong comes swiftly. Traditional stock ownership is fraught with wrong guesses, too, but it also offers the comforting element of time to erase the mistake with appreciation. America is filled with patient millionaires who would have lost it all years ago as short sellers.

At the same time, short selling is a necessary component of market systems. It pushes markets toward higher efficiency by adding added selling pressures. It's not bad or evil. But very aggressive.

Bear Funds in All Their Varieties

These are mutual funds or pools of money that short sell, buy hedges, or options. They may buy derivatives. Essentially, they buy assets which aim to benefit from tremendous volatility or downward markets. Again, very aggressive, but serving a purpose for both the markets and certain investors.

☞ *Aggressive Strategies during the Wealth Shift*

During the Wealth Shift, we *may* experience a significant fall in the stock market. But that's just too precise a prediction for this format and at this time. What is more predictable is a protracted period of advances and declines, over and over for a decade or more. Consistent growth and a matching stock price will be difficult for many, many companies to sustain. That's an ideal environment for short selling and other aggressive strategies. You'll see it happening. You may also want to get involved. Use caution, but don't rule it out if you're tolerance for risk is high and your time horizon is distant.

Chapter 6
Preparing for the Wealth Shift

The cherished notion of one's "golden years" has probably only been attainable for small segment of Americans—people born between 1900 and 1940. It wasn't even possible for all but a fraction of people born before 1900. And for those on the late end of the curve, it's been as much myth as reality.

Sure, plenty of those folks have grabbed the gold watch and played shuffleboard in the sunset. But at least as many others have found themselves, by choice or circumstance, working well into their "postworking" lives. Many continued in their lifetime work, started consulting businesses, or found alternative part-time jobs because they hadn't saved enough money to live in the way they'd been used to. And it looks like this trend is going to continue.

A recent piece in the *New York Times* cited surveys by AARP and other organizations that found up to 80 percent of baby boomers plan to do some sort of paid work into their seventies. They see continued participation in the workforce as a way to help them stay mentally sharp and socially engaged, as well as financially more secure.

Clearly, for most baby boomers, this isn't going to be their father's retirement.

John Mellencamp as Retirement Advisor

Let's say you keep working into your seventies, then what? The rocker John Mellencamp saw the world many retirees will be inhabiting in his 1988 classic "Jack & Diane": "Life goes on long after the thrill of livin' is gone." While Mr. Mellencamp probably wasn't talking about the unrelenting advancements in medicine and science, he might as well have. We are going to be living longer, perhaps dramatically longer.

In his highly recommended book, *Inevitable Surprises*, Peter Schwartz, the well-regarded futurist, anticipates an America where the healthy one-hundred-year-old is common and the outer limits of longevity are extended even longer. Think one hundred and ten is impossible? What about one hundred and fifteen? Whether or not gene-based therapies deliver as advertised, you can almost certainly count on a longer retirement than your parents had or are having.

So while you're doing all that extra living, maybe as much as forty or fifty years' worth, what's funding it? You might not be working for all those decades, but you'll be livin'. (And how are you going afford the thrills?)

Think of this chapter as the book's workbook. This is where your situation—your assets, your challenges, your dreams—intersect with the predicted new realities of the Wealth Shift. To give you a clearer sense of the potential of your future in the Wealth Shift world, I've crafted a series of scenarios, based on real-life situations to help you address the risks and challenges faced by different demographic groups. Inevitably, you will find yourself falling into one of the following four subsets, or a logical combination of them.

However, before you start to pigeonhole yourself into one group or another, I offer the following universal wisdoms that apply to almost everyone, no matter what your age, stage, economic, or investing profile.

Note for Growth Investors

The younger investor with twenty or more years to retirement has several choices to make. The first is to decide what kind of retiree from the above list you want to be, then invest to get there. It is the same investment model, with different investments.

What Dad Said:
Advice Strong Enough to Endure the Wealth Shift

Imagine the kind of retirement you want to have, do the math, get a plan, begin. Oh, and let me give you the same advice my dad gave me: Buy low. Sell high.

Simplistic? Sure. But not as simple as it sounds. It's about balancing a portfolio and rebalancing it with detached maturity. It's the best piece of advice anyone can give you. Include it in your portfolio of wisdom. Here's how to do it.

"Low" is associated with anxiety and fear, feelings that keep investors on the sidelines. "High" comes with exhilaration and few if any signs of a fall. Investors tend to want more highs and fewer lows, but lows will always be a part of every portfolio. Something will always be up, something will always be down, or flat. The problem is, even if someone has the gut to buy at the low, they almost never have the foresight to sell at the high. I equate foresight with crystal balls: they're both bunk. What's required is the discipline to buy whatever is low and to sell whatever is high at regular intervals.

Let's divide the world into two investments: Investment Alpha and Investment Beta. We decide we're going to own fifty percent in Alpha and fifty percent in Beta. We have $200 total and put $100 in each. Alpha doubles to $200. Beta drops by half to $50. We now have $250 dollars. You just made twenty-five percent, that's great. But now eighty percent of your money is in a single investment, Alpha, that can be dangerous. And yet, what does the average investor do now? Dump Beta and buys more Alpha. They just sold low and bought high. Dad would not approve.

The disciplined investor takes the profits from Alpha and buys more Beta to bring the portfolio back in balance, that is, with $125 in each. "Beta's day will come," says the savvy investor. This investor has just bought low and sold high. And he didn't ask whether he should or shouldn't. He didn't try to outguess the market.

Every month, or every quarter or every year, we rebalance back to the portions set in advance. Those portions can change, of course, but the decision to change those is based on long-term performance and investment goals, not monthly performance. Will it be the absolute high every time you sell? No, but you can't always guess that, anyway. But over time, you will be selling your high, above the halfway mark, for every asset and you will be buying at below the halfway mark for every asset—again and again, with no emotion, right on schedule.

I've seen one asset allocation scenario based on the simple principle above, and it shows a three hundred sixty percent return between 1961 and 1981. This was a period when the Dow was up only a few percent and the long-term bond went from three percent to seventeen percent. The allocation reflected large-cap stocks and small-cap stocks and bonds in roughly fifty percent equity and fifty percent bonds. There is an emotion that goes with this very unemotional model: elation.

Growth or Income

The issue of growth and income is a thread woven throughout this book, and now it's time to grab a hold of it. If you're a growth investor with a fifteen-to-thirty-year retirement threshold, I'll keep it short: buy what the boomers will want, and that's income-producing instruments. The bonds and dividend-paying equities are going to be trading higher as demand drives their value up. Buy them and wait. (It's all in chapter 5). Living the Wealth Shift is going to challenge current or soon-to-be income investors the most—those boomers with fifteen years or less until retirement-so the balance of this chapter is devoted to those of you in this demographic. See if you can find yourself in one of the following scenarios.

1. The Well-Prepared Retiree: A lifetime of wise investing has paid off for this group, but there are challenges. Overconfidence can lead them to keep playing it big in equities when they should rebuild their portfolio around income. And perhaps one of the sharpest risks they face is what got them in the advantageous position they are in.

2. The Early Retiree: This group will be self-funding until Social Security or other retirement savings kick in. But they are an active group with a higher burn rate for their cash. The main risk they face is spending their liquid assets too soon and having to tap their qualified assets. That's money gone for good, and they might have decades left to live. Inflation is also a risk here, too—over the years, even low rates of inflation can cut into buying power. Since this group has simply added more nonearning years to their years of living, they could see inflation eating into their well-planned nest egg at a rate they did not anticipate.

3. The Pensioner: These folks are the last of a breed who usually retire at sixty-five with the fixed benefits from a pension fund as well as Social Security or other annuitized assets. This combination can make for comfortable living, but there are risks. The fixed income doesn't give them much tolerance for increasing costs and inflation. And as the headlines attest, corporate pension funds are not secured in the vault at Ft. Knox; they are at the mercy of a continually fluid corporate ownership and leadership.

4. On Your Own: These are the hardworking Americans with 401(k)s and IRAs—but are these enough? Social Security in whatever form won't cover their expenses. This group will probably keep working well past sixty-five. The low-rate environment of Wealth Shift could hit this group hardest, as they'll be depending on their saved assets to continue to generate income.

5. Last-Minute Saver: All pre-retirees might think of themselves as members of this group. The kids may be out on their own, the house may be paid off—the pressure is still on. Even the most optimistic are clearly seeing the implications of their lack of planning. Their challenges are many, including the tendency to take larger investment risks in an attempt to catch up.

The situations that follow do not offer off-the-shelf solutions. They provide starting points for the process of developing your own plan of action.

1. WELL-PREPARED RETIREE

"Congratulations! Now watch out." That's my message to these folks who have succeeded where most don't, and have enough financial assets to retire comfortably. Here's who they are, and why I urge caution.

Who:	Married couple, both sixty-two years old
Situation:	On the edge of retirement, or just retired
Assets:	Three million dollar total in mostly liquid assets, probably a qualified plan that can be distributed at any time. The house up north has been sold and the profits distributed to the existing portfolio and to purchase a condo on the Gulf Coast
Needs:	$100,000 annually from now until . . . ?
Strategies:	Buy and hold for the income. Opportunistic sales from a well-balanced portfolio with disciplined rebalancing

In Practice

These folks may be in the low end of the well-prepared group, but with a disciplined approach, they'll be just fine. The approach here is a mix of solid income and classic asset allocation.

The income is the easy part. We take $2 million and invest long term for consistent income. They'll need 5 percent to do it, but that's possible to lock in, especially in the early days of the Wealth Shift, or better yet, now. That's their $100K to live on each year. Now let's put the other million to work.

That money will fund a second portfolio—a balanced group of investments that might include stocks and bonds, cash, and maybe some real estate. For simplicity, we'll call them A, B, and C. They are portioned in the portfolio at a third each. At regular intervals— quarterly, twice a year, annually—these three components will be rebalanced. During these intervals any one of those asset classes will be likely to showing gains. Let's say asset A goes up twenty percent, asset B stays flat, and asset C goes down twenty percent. So, in that period, the well-prepared retiree sells the twenty percent of asset A and put it in to investment C, which is declining. They just bought low and sold high. Grains can be plowed back into the million, or can be used to fund the extras, be it a few weeks on the beach or new tires for the Hummer . . .

Portions of the second portfolio can be quite speculative, or solidly safe. The most important thing is to spread the risk across several investment types, set the proportions to match their tolerance for risk, and rebalance with unemotional discipline.

Risk? Some. The portfolio can stay flat, or lose in all portions, but that's the nature of investing. However, with a well-balanced group, the overall losses are going to be a short-term dip in a steadily growing set of assets. Remember the boy playing with the yo-yo as he walked up the mountain—you can watch the yo-yo or watch the mountain. Keep your eye on the mountain here, but there is one very high cliff to stay away from—the urge to maximize returns.

People in this group probably got where they are with some aggressive investing, so there's a temptation to ask themselves, why stop now? I have about forty reasons, one for every year you'll be living in retirement.

Set your yearly budget, orient your portfolio to deliver precisely that, and then leave it alone. You may think you can get 7 percent instead of 5 percent, but you might think wrong. If your portfolio gives you room to play, as in the above scenario, go have fun, but don't put your retirement at risk because you couldn't dial back your aggressiveness. Save it for the golf course.

One final thought on discipline: When your job is to spend money, you can get very good at it. I've seen people retire with $4 or $6 million and then proceed to upgrade the home, the fleet, and the vacation schedule, all the while burning through a several hundred thousand a year. Classic overconfidence. A few years later comes a wake-up call that says loud and clear, "Unless you want to go back to work, slow down."

2. EARLY RETIREE

Here's some good news: You don't need millions to retire early. If you have some assets now, and some income you can count on later . . . and you are prepared to live within a comfortable but modest budget, you can start early. Here's how.

Who: Married couple, both fifty-five years old
Situation: Ten years until a modest pension kicks in and gains from real estate can be realized, but ready to stop working now
Assets: $880,000 total
Needs: $60,000 annually until sixty-five, $20,000 annually after sixty-five when pensions/Social Security pay $40,000 annually
Strategies: $600,000 into a ladder now, $280,000 invested to earn five percent annually over the next ten years

In Practice

These fortunate folks are both fifty-five years old, and can live on about $60,000 a year until sixty-five when a pension and Social

Security kicks in. Those benefits will give them $40,000 a year, which means they only need an extra $20,000 a year in income from their portfolio after age sixty-five.

We're going to take $600,000 and divide it into ten $60,000 blocks. That's our ladder, stretching through the decade ahead. Each $60K is invested in bonds or CDs that will mature in subsequent years, the first in one year, the second in two years, etc. With each maturity, they take back the $60K for living and invest the interest in a separate instrument along with the balance of their assets.

To some, burning the principal to live on so early is heresy, but it's simply one of two options. They have to live on something, and they can either consume principal or consume interest. And the pension and Social Security give them the option of consuming principal, so they are. They are more comfortable knowing they have $60,000 every year than they are with the uncertainty of interest-based income. Not a bad choice for the Wealth Shift.

So every January 1st, these folks get paid for the year. They can live with that. They also take comfort in knowing their ladder will generate $230,000 over the course of a decade. That cash goes straight to work with their other $280,000 from their original assets at age fifty-five for approximately $705,000 to supplement the $40,000 they'll be earning at retirement. If they hit their portfolio for just $20K a year, and it keeps earning 5 percent, they'll have enough to live on well past one hundred. That's forty-five plus years in retirement. Good for them.

The upside? No worries. That first ten years of retirement is on autopilot, as long as they keep reinvesting the interest earned off the ladder.

The risks? Many. It might be tempting to start cannibalizing the interest off that ladder. After all, they are still young and active and there is Europe to explore. Or maybe one of their kids needs some money to start a business. It takes discipline here to stay the course.

Inflation is a risk as well—as the years accumulate, inflation can reduce buying power while they're still buying as much as before. But with a good plan, and a disciplined advisor, they have lots to look forward to.

3. PENSIONER

The few, the proud, the last of their kind. Years of service in the military, government, education, or on a Detroit assembly line pays off with a nice pension. Liquidity could be a problem; here's what they can do.

Who: Married couple, both sixty-five years old, former government workers
Situation: Just retired
Assets: Two pensions paying a total of $70,000 annually, $450,000 in other saved assets
Needs: $80,000 annually
Strategies: Buy and hold for income. Opportunistic sales from a well-balanced portfolio with disciplined rebalancing

In Practice

This hardworking couple just needs $10K more after their pensions each year to live comfortably. That's easy: take $200K and buy and hold long-term bonds at five percent. There's $10K a year to complete their needs, and $250K ready to keep in play. You guessed it, in a well-balanced portfolio that is rebalanced with ruthless discipline.

For these folks, this second set of assets is particularly important because it represents all the liquidity they have. If they come across an opportunity or an immediate and urgent need for cash, they'll have some. They're fortunate, because many pensioners don't—their pension IS their portfolio, but with trends in pension management, that's changing, too.

Lump-sum payouts are almost always on the table now for pensioners, especially those from private industry or education. It's usually a fair amount, too, maybe even a premium. I typically advise people to take it because it will give them options as well as peace of mind.

A lump sum invested wisely can give you income and liquidity. And it comes into your control, not the pension fund's. These funds are running out of money, or will be soon, as the boomers retire and drag rates down just as the checks are going out. I'm not in the pension fund business, but I have to believe their actuaries are getting jumpy as they watch modern medicine and good living extend the lives of their pensioners past what they guessed a decade ago.

The pressure is on to create returns, now more than ever, and you can see it in the way these fund managers try to move markets and even shove around the companies they're invested in. It's their job, and they do it with gusto, which may more and more look like desperation. Hence the eagerness to pay out lump sums. Once you're out of the fund, your assets are lost, too, but it's one less long, long, long retirement that needs to be funded.

For the people who elect to stay and have confidence in the long-term viability of the fund, there are still risks. One is personal, one is economic.

At a personal level, they need to create and stick to a realistic budget. The fixed nature of their income virtually demands it.

Economically, the rising cost of living (otherwise known as inflation) can kill them with a thousand tiny cuts. Most pensions don't have periodic adjustments for cost of living, which means pensioners have to adjust their spending. During the Wealth Shift, when inflation will likely be low or absent, it might not be much of a concern. But it won't last forever, and inflation will return as a fact of life. A two percent inflation rate endured over forty years of retirement is worse than five percent over a relatively short retirement sprint of ten years.

4. ON THEIR OWN

This is a big group because, by definition, it can include people who could be anywhere in the age, income, or demographic curves. What unites them is their sole reliance on assets they have generated and saved. No pensions. Minimal Social Security. They are on their own, but that doesn't mean they are out of options.

Who: Married couple, both sixty
Situation: Still working, hoping to retire at sixty-five
Assets: A projected total of $700,000 in two 401(k)s and $300,000 in other liquid assets
Needs: Salaries are sufficient now. Retirement needs unknown
Strategies: Plan. Save. Identify the gaps in what their assets can generate and what they need to live on

In Practice

These folks are feeling pretty confident, but I'm here to hang a cloud over their rosy scenario with three simple words: Do the math. A million bucks sounds like a lot of money at first, but the $700K is really $500K after the taxes are paid at disbursement. And the real total of $800K is only going to generate $40K annually if it's getting five percent. What now?

The first thing is they need to be aware of the income they can generate ($40K) and determine if that's enough to live on. Hint: It's not. Let's say they need $50K at a minimum and would love to get $60K. They're $10K to $20K in the hole already, but at least they stopped patting themselves on the back long enough to make some calculations.

Some of their options: Keep working and saving with a new perspective on what they'll need. They can also change their investment strategy to reflect a new tolerance for risk that comes with a rapid growth mind-set. It's a tough choice, because they're putting the very assets they need so much in a more vulnerable position. A balanced portfolio can have an aggressive tilt. That's understandable, but so is regular and periodic rebalancing. Sound familiar? Great, tell your neighbor; it's a good mantra for so many Americans who, like the folks in this scenario, are on their own.

5. LAST-MINUTE SAVER

Who: Married couple, fifty-eight and sixty-four. One child out of college
Situation: Recent empty-nesters, no college to fund anymore, still working
Assets: Minimal—$80,000 equity in a home—$100,000 in two IRAs
Needs: Undetermined
Strategies: Determine their retirement expenses and begin living on that now. Set a realistic retirement time threshold and save aggressively

In Practice

Sadly, millions of Americans can see themselves in the above profile. Maybe a few of them picked up *Wealth Shift*, so here's what I'd say to them: Practice being retired.

That doesn't mean stop working; it means start living on what they think—at a minimum—retirement will cost. If they think they can get by in retirement on $50K a year, start living on that now, even if they're making $100K. Two good things will happen. One, they'll confront the reality of retirement, which is something they've been unwilling or unable to do in the abstract. And two, they're saving $50K a year.

If the house has topped out in terms of value, sell it and downscale. Get into a small home in a growing area or maybe even a cheap apartment. Plow every penny of equity into the well-balanced, regularly rebalanced portfolio you're getting tired of hearing me preach about. Same with the yearly savings. It's a race to the finish now. So where is the finish?

They need to set a retirement age that allows them to keep saving as long as possible, let's say when the last one turns seventy, which would be twelve years. Assuming they've been able to sock away $50K each of those years, that's a $600,000 principal, plus what their other assets have been able to generate in a dozen years of disciplined investing and in an appreciating home market. They might just have a million dollars. At five percent annually, they have their $50K a year to keep living in the manner to which they've become accustomed.

Was it easy? Hell, no. But was there any other choice? Not really, short of moving in with the kid or the shelter. And don't say "lottery." These folks have already been living in a kind of dream world. We don't need to be making it even sillier.

Don't Go It Alone

This isn't a pitch for my financial advisor brethren. That said, you're going to need some help. The low interest rates, driven by millions of retiring boomers becoming lenders and not borrowers, is going to confound even the advisors who see it coming.

Regardless of whether your advisor buys the Wealth Shift scenario whole, he or she certainly sees the looming Boomer retirement, and it's simply intuitive to anticipate a migration (or a stampede) away from equities and into fixed-return assets. So ask your advisor about generating income in a low-rate environment, where higher yielding bonds are scarce and banks are begging to loan you some of the cash getting dusty in their vaults. See if they have an income-producing investment model that's designed for a five percent rate environment, or even lower. If not, keep shopping. You're buying their discipline. Make them show you what it is. Final thought here: I don't manage my own investments. I know I can be emotional about my own money, and I'm in the business of being unemotional about money. So get some help.

Final Words

Wealth Shift contains investment predictions and guidance that have been developed and sharpened over my life as a business historian and my career as an investment educator and advisor. I'm firmly convinced that these forward-looking ideas will come to pass in a form and in a sequence very similar to how they are presented in this book. It's my sincere hope that the strategies contained in *Wealth Shift* are the starting points for your own investigation.

Wealth Shift is intentionally broad in its scope, so I urge you to consult with your financial advisors about your individual situation and specific goals. While every person's financial situation is unique, one thing is certain: over 70 million baby boomers are moving toward retirement and life as elderly citizens in the United States. Every sensible investor is looking toward that period with anxiousness, if not outright fear. With *Wealth Shift* I attempted to replace the uncertainty with concrete understanding and a menu of approaches one might take to prepare and prosper. I congratulate you for your diligence in reading, and wish you good fortune in the difficult years ahead.

Notes